NOBODY CARES NO ONES COMING

Practical wisdom to stop sabotaging
your relationships, backed up
by real-life experience.

Good Cop and Bad Cop

GCBC
COACHING

Book Cover, "Whiskey Road" by Bad Cop First edition 2022

ISBN-13: 979-8-9872552-0-9 eBook
ISBN-13: 979-8-9872552-1-6 Paperback
ISBN-13: 979-8-9872552-2-3 Hardcover

Printed in the United States of America

CONTENTS

PREFACE

"Own Your Shit!"

Real expectations

Real effort

Actual results

Positive change…

INTRODUCTION

"The truth will set you free, but first it will piss you off."

- Gloria Steinem

Yes, we know who Gloria Steinem is, and we are not fans of her platform, but give credit where credit is due. This is the most correct statement that she has ever uttered, and we are not above using it for whatever purpose it applies. Though Ms. Steinem will not agree with this material, the facts are facts. She and drones of like-minded people have had their chance for the last sixty-plus years, and you have noticed that the changes have not worked out so well.

We will not take you through a litany of stats and figures to make a point. Others have done this, and you live in an age of infinite information. We have amassed a wealth of knowledge through experience in dating, relationships, marriage, fatherhood, multiple careers, and coaching. Through all this experience, failure has been our best resource.

"Success consists of going from failure to failure without loss of enthusiasm."

- Winston Churchill

This learning curve and insight into the functioning of western society and how society has affected relationships can aid you and those around you to live happy and fulfilling lives. The actual cost is your time and effort.

The value of the type of information, continuous flow of information, and to whom this information is shared, and discussed is critical. This is the greatest gift we can provide to one another. We have also gained knowledge from reading and putting into practice wisdom from others, some of the note are:

Kevin Samuels

Jordan Peterson

Rollo Tomassi

Rich Cooper

Rian Stone

Stephan Aarnio

Greg Adams

All the above authors are recommended reading for future motivation, different wisdom, and perspectives. Most have YouTube channels or Podcasts that update regularly so that you can listen to or watch at your leisure.

Consider us, and the list above as the Male Mentor figures in your life. The father figures that teach you the true ways of the world. We once belonged to socially acceptable Men's Clubs and other groups that aided in our support and development. These were amazingly effective for sharing and passing information on life's problems, sharing notes, and gaining valuable knowledge through the experience of other men. There seems to be a need for this since most men of today and those up-and-comers have been raised in a single-mother household or raised in a home with a present but absent father who supplied little guidance in leadership, masculinity, relationship building, and maintenance.

We will give you the absolute truth as we have experienced it, and guidance on how to prevent or correct the situations that you put yourself into. Yes, you have either put yourself into or have done nothing to this point to improve these situations, or perhaps have seen little to no results.

Historically speaking, young boys were raised by seeing other men. These day-to-day operations weren't only limited to instructional in value. They were of leading a household, protecting them, mentoring all who presided within them. After a necessary amount of time, the boys were released into the world. Recently, society has conditioned us to believe that men are not needed to raise children other than the financial aspects that they can provide. It is also believed that only women, children, and pets are loved unconditionally. A man is only allowed to be loved based on his ability to provide.

Historically, during those 20 years that the boy is seeing the older male role models, especially through the adolescent or teen years, the man is teaching him things that will shape the rest of his life. Often done in a covert manner of observation with little actual verbal instruction taking place. This could be a reason others view this especially important aspect of male training as unnecessary.

The male role model also provides this for his daughter just by her seeing the interaction between her father and mother, she gains the knowledge of what a masculine male should be. She can also see how the mother can use manipulation or coercion to affect her father's reaction to developmental growth. Her observation of her father will set the standard for men for the rest of her life and help her with the vetting process of future love interests, something we will cover in future portions of the material.

We will emphasize the interaction and observations of the male role model in the pages of this book. This truthful information may offend, insult, or anger you. That is what a male role model's responsibility is as a mentor, give the truth, you need to hear, or in this case, read it. A good role model will always hold a mirror up to the world and correct misinformation or misunderstanding.

You will want to argue, it is only human nature to stay comfortable, but if that was working, you wouldn't be looking for answers. Sometimes you need another male opinion, which may seem harsh, although highly influential.

Personal responsibility and bold action to correct what you lack is the only way to make a better life. Lofty standards of life are not obtained through shortcuts, excuses, or laziness. Other men with lofty standards can aid you with your journey. Nobody Cares No Ones Coming has a voice willing and able to give you continuous guidance in future podcasts and added volumes of future reading material.

Take what we give you and use it as you see fit. You are the one who must live with the consequences of your choices. You may love or hate what we say, either way, we give the right insight backed by experience and facts. We don't care how you feel about the words written here; we have zero fucks to give. You are the only one who can affect true positive change in your life. This is accomplished through you changing your mindset and acting accordingly.

YOUR FRAGILE FEELINGS

"Golden sticks and stones may break my bones, but words will never hurt me."

-   Alexander Kinglake, 1830

Society has programmed us to fear offending anyone in the recent past (40 years or so), due to this you have been told half-truths with a very soft-handed approach. Unbelievably, this is to your detriment. If you do not hear and accept criticism from others, you cannot improve. This is a necessity, as others can see around your potential blind spots. Worse still, you have been told that you are great just the way you are, and to just be yourself. This is a complete and utter falsehood. If we were to apply that thinking to other aspects of life, why would we have to obtain an education? Couldn't you just wing it and get a couple of letters after your name and a high-paying career?

Or the worst lie of them all, "Big is Beautiful". This one is an absolute atrocity to public health. It has been proven repeatedly through countless medical studies that the largest issue in the western world is obesity. It has destroyed our health care system by focusing on all the other diseases that come with obesity.

The healthcare system, pharmaceutical manufactures, and fitness industry can hardly keep up with the demand for their services. Media outlets bombard the public with falsehoods, saying it's ok to be obese. This mentality does nothing to hold people accountable, it is safe and inclusive, which generates higher ratings. It boggles the mind that medical professionals are ignored by media outlets, giving you false impressions, all for the mighty dollar.

The other side of the coin is the "Heroin Model" years of rail-thin women who appeared to be so emaciated, that they would place themselves in harm's way during normal intercourse. Our DNA has programmed us to be attracted to a healthy-looking woman to better ensure healthy offspring. Neither the "Big is Beautiful" nor the "Heroin Model" fit this bill.

You may point the finger at the capitalist system, the government for not regulating the food industry, or other whack job ideas. Why must someone else correct our inability to push ourselves away from the table filled with the least nutritious food that money can buy? Where has all the personal responsibility gone?

We must tone down our language, tell half-truths, or just outright lie to prevent someone's feelings from being hurt and unleashing the wrath of the army of hateful people. That wrath can be very troublesome to deal with and it can cost you everything. Your career, life savings, relationships, and even your marriage.

All because you said something factual backed up with scientific evidence, with the intent for improvement. What a ridiculous concept that intent no longer matters.

The quote to start this chapter was originally published in 1830, a time when offending people was not a crucifiable offense. It was intended to increase resiliency among people so that society could improve to better things, by doing what is hard. Even Wikipedia, states that it is intended to defend bullying, what a crock of shit. What do you expect when the content is allowed to be edited by anyone? We have lost this throughout time, and it is now, hopefully, due for a resurgence.

It has become a time when people are no longer capable of taking an honest look in the mirror and correcting faults. Heaven forbids anyone else to point something out in that mirror or even hold one up for you, as they are just as guilty of saying the sad things that hurt you and everyone gets a trophy for just showing up.

You can't even have a mutual conversation that could be offensive to others that may overhear it. What is worse is, with modern technology, sound bites can be taken from multiple podcasts or videos and spliced together without context, and you're the bad person. I can think of Dave Chappelle and Joe Rogan being two examples of this in recent history.

Both managed the situations very differently, one refusing to cave, the other apologizing. Translation, one kept his dignity and stuck to his guns, and the other sold out because his livelihood (sponsorships and platform) was in peril all because strangers were offended.

FUCK THAT...

The world doesn't give a rat's ass about your feelings. "Nobody Cares, No Ones coming to help."

ABSOLUTELY NO ONE.

The barista with the great perky tits who winks at you when she hands you your daily dose of diabetic inducting unicorn shit sprinkled latte as you throw a fiver in the tip jar is using you because the wink worked the first time. She doesn't care about you, only your money.

Any one you may be sending money to, or liking her Instagram pictures, you better believe she is not going to shed a single tear for you if you need her help. The simpleton behavior you previously displayed when you give her your attention has told her it is acceptable to manipulate you.

Brian was an alcoholic and homeless when I met him. He set continuous patterns of self-deprecating behavior by finding girls online as girl friends in foreign countries and would send them money. It got so bad that even after he found out his first girl was a part of a call center group, set up to lure weak men like Brian in and get them to send money, he still went to the same dating site and started the same routine with another girl.

The relationship wasn't real; however, the instant "empathy" and human connection were, at least for him.

He was drunk, homeless, living out of his car, sleeping in his excrement, and suicidal. "She" knew it and still took money from him. The truth of it is, deep down inside Brian knew it as well. He went through four girls in the Philippines and $20,000 before he would have an epiphany, that he was the problem. The money kept someone on the other end of the phone, for the human connection. Sad, however, this story is played out hundreds of thousands of times daily throughout the world.

The feelings are never reciprocated in these types of "relationships". There was always an excuse to not meet. Always an excuse to keep sending money. The relationship was not real. Hell, some may have a similar experience and can sympathize with you. But you better believe, they are not going to stop what they are doing to crawl into that whole with you. So go ahead and cry a river, then build a bridge and get the fuck over it.

If you can't control your emotions in front of others, you are a fucking toddler throwing a tantrum. A tantrum because your ice cream fell off its cone and onto the floor, which is your fault because you didn't hold it properly. This can be entertaining for an observer, as Jared Keeso says, "Fuck, I can watch kids fall off bikes all day. I don't give a shit about your kids".

You, however, are a "functioning" adult. If you can't control your Fee Fees (feelings) and must act on every one of them with great intensity, you need some stoicism in your life. "But I don't know what that means". Look that shit up, we are not holding you by the hand.

The absolute first and most important thing you must come to grips with is that if something is giving you bad fee fees, you are in control of how you react to that. You can either emote, whine, or complain, or you can physically do something productive and take some fucking action to turn the bad fee fees into good fee fees.

Taking ownership is crucial to future success, you are the only one who could better your situation. It is the first step in improving the situation. To do this you must stop making excuses or trying to lay blame on others. This action prevents you from taking responsibility for the consequences that you are now facing.

Ownership is the hardest step to overcome due to the social conditioning that you have suffered. There is no such thing as safety without strong, competent, and violent people to control the borders. When the barbarians are at the gates, Ms. History of Basket Weaving, PhD, and Mr. Liberal Science, DLS is not going to be able to stop them. Don't be them. If you believe that you are safe without those violent people, your reality is not a true representation of the real world.

This is referred to a Safe World Theory, and people who think this way are also known as Victims.

This concept is perfectly summed up by Jack Nicholas in the movie A Few Good Men. "You don't want the truth because deep down in places you don't talk about at parties, you want me on that wall -- you need me on that wall.". The movie does well to show you how there are only small sections of black and white, and a much larger area of grey. Most people operate in that grey area.

Your safety has a cost. This cost is paid by others who have the ability for violence and chose to control it for the greater good. Understand that this is not as simple as it may seem. The ability for violence of a soldier and the murderer is the same. The only difference is the soldier is controlled; the murderer is not. You can either be a part of the problem or apart of the solution, either way, both may call for violence. Own the fact that you can't be violent when it calls for it or that you do not have good control of when and how to use your violent ability and fix that shit.

The recent events on college campuses of creating safe

spaces for a particular group is a perfect example of Safe World Theory. The organizers of the spaces do not understand that they exist only because people with more power (strength, masculinity, etc.) don't care enough about it to stop it. They think that their words are enough to stop an opposing group from running ram shot over their lines. Laws are another example of this, all laws are enforced by more powerful people (police, lawyers, judges) than the individual who faces the consequences. The only reason they are allowed to exist, or the western government at all for that matter, is that the military (a stronger force than even law enforcement) allows it to happen.

When you make excuses, place blame, whine, bitch, or complain about a situation, you are taking the victim mentality. The danger of the victim mentality is that it absolves you of any responsibility. This prevents you from changing. Otherwise known as, learning from your mistakes. You must own the issue, find the cause, and fucking fix it.

For example:

You are in an unhappy marriage with a nagging beast of a wife.

-       Fix it. Raise your Sexual Market Value (SMV) and Relationship Market Value (RMV), covered in depth later. Sprinkle in a little Masculine Alpha Energy and start passing shit tests. Also start leading the household better, by fixing the shit around the house before she starts nagging (your damn job, btw) will work wonders in this area.

You are divorced and on the dating scene and the only

kind of woman you can pull in are single moms in your age group that don't appeal to you long-term.

- Fix it. Raise your SMV by going to the Iron Church (Gym) and praying (pick up heavy shit and put it down, repeatedly and consistently). This will raise your attractiveness to the other sex, allowing you to pull from a lower age bracket which may grant you better long-term success. While you are doing that, start peacocking (dressing better) to show off the added SMV.

Your wife of 10 years is dryer than the Sahara.

- Fix it. There is a reason the woman, who used to bang you in a manner that would make a Porn Star blush three nights a week, but that was eight years ago, and she has stopped. If you are a fat, lazy ass, get off the couch and lose the weight by picking heavy shit up and putting it down. Get a hobby that doesn't revolve around the family, preferably something in combat sports (multiple birds, single stone). This can raise your attraction and masculine levels in the SMV and the protect aspect of the RMV and get the Gina tingles raging again.

Stan saw himself at 50 years old with it all figured out, or so he thought. His house was in the right location and the right size. The grocery getter was paid for and rebuilt recently. The truck, motorcycle, (Soft Tail Heritage classic), and boat were all but paid off. Hell, he even had a full head of hair. He retired early with enough income to keep the ship afloat each month with just a small nest egg.

He also had a beautiful family and a few close friends. However, his relationship with his spouse went cold shortly after he retired early.

Why?

He at once lost sexual and relationship market value, by cutting off his job market value with the retirement at an early age.

He lost that value because he stopped showing growth and productivity. He stopped exercising and became less attractive, overall, less enticing to his spouse. The arguments ensued and excuses were formed to continue to shirk from responsibilities. He was taking a break! That's fine for a while. What she saw was a man on the couch day in and day out, just a shell of his former self. She was doing her thing and she reverted to how most women think, why am I doing everything around the house?

The truth is she doesn't care about your previous accomplishments. She doesn't care the lights are on and the fridge is full. Internally she is settled by continuous growth. She is reassured by it. She values it as sexual market value. Yes, our sexual and relationship market value is not only based on overall appearance, but also valued by being highly productive and continued growth as well.

Stan unwittingly gave up all the power in the relationship by resting on his laurels. He wrapped his masculine energy with a bow and gifted it to his wife. She viewed his "break" as a sign of things to come. She feared that she would have to be the future bread winner, even though his retirement was plenty to keep the house and family living comfortably for the foreseeable future. None of this mattered to her, she was working, and he wasn't.

Yes, he's retired, did everything right, and worked his ass off for 30 years in a dangerous profession on top of it all. It wasn't enough. The hard truth of it is you are not allowed to go dormant at 50, or at any age for that matter. You may never be allowed to go dormant. If you want to keep this woman and be happy with her, maintain your frame, and have a healthy relationship, you can't go dormant and sit at home scrolling on the phone from the couch.

You're a single guy in your teens or twenties thrown in the friendzone by countless love interests.

- Fix it. Know that you are in the friend zone because you lack SMV and have too much RMV, for that girl/woman. Pray at the Iron Church to bring up the attractiveness aspect. For god's sake, stop participating in comfort tests. If you are not in a relationship (we question at that age why you would even want to be), you do not need to be providing comfort to any woman who provides nothing to you, but "friendship". At that age you don't need female friends (more on Fuck Buddies later), you need some crazy monkey sex so you can gain valuable experience that your future long-term love interest can benefit from.

If you are a woman who has seen your husband slowly turn into a jiggly mass of his former self that you can walk all over, and let's be honest here, you hate the very sight of him.

- Fix it. Before you run out and find a willing Chad

McHorsecock (his middle name is Filthy) to lay some pipe so that you can feel something again, you know, like the sexual creature that everyone is. Give your husband this book, or others from the reading list and if he understands the wisdom, just stay out of his way while he fixes the issues and runs his plan. Also, you should wait for the improvements before you go out and fill the void that a lazy husband has created. If he gets it, he will come back better than the man you married. What's a little more patience for you anyway, and wouldn't be nice not to have to take care of a grown child anymore?

A strange thing starts to happen when one spouse starts busting their ass to get their shit together, the other spouse usually wants to do it too. Typically, around the time that people in the wild start to take notice of the improvements. You two go out to dinner and the waitress starts to flirt. The wife takes notice and will equate the new interest to his raised SMV. However, preselection is also at work here. This feeling she has is known as dread.

Dread is a very powerful "medication", if you take it as directed, it will improve the health of the relationship. Too much and it can kill it, much like a morphine overdose. A partner should always try to have a slow drip of constant dread in the other partner, and it should go without saying that what causes dread should never be acted upon.

The person with the most options or cares less about the other partner has control of the relationship. A study that took place between 2009 to 2015 showed that 70% of divorces are initiated by the wife. Also, a survey in 2014 found that 50% of women have a backup man or "plan B" if the current relationship fails. 20% of those surveyed admitted that the backup was a "friend" of their partner. Know that she, just by being a woman has a constant covert drip of dread.

Remember, that dread is a two-way street, the bubble in your gut as you watch another man hit on her, is not gas, it's dread. No reason to club him over the head, it's just his DNA telling him to get a baby inside her. If you are the high-value man, operating at his best, she won't give a flying fuck who this pissant is.

It is most common to start seeing "sabotage" attempts as a natural reaction to a slow overdose of dread. Once you start raising your SMV, you may come home to a kitchen full of junk food or freshly baked cookies.

This is a shit test and a comfort test wrapped with a little bow. Understand the shit portion of this is she is attempting to sabotage your progress and to divert you from the path by testing your discipline. The comfort portion of this is the underlying cause of the shit test, to begin with. You are outpacing her SMV improvement, she has not started to improve, or doesn't want to do the work. She may also be using the classic; "I don't want to get big" excuse to lift weights. She will only see improvements in her bust/waist/hip ratio by doing so.

You should provide a little comfort (maybe eat one cookie, then take the rest to work for all the other shlubs), but you should never stop what you're doing in raising your SMV or RMV. Stay the course if it still shows improvement, and never let someone else dictate your actions for their happiness.

A bonus point is by taking the rest of the cookies to work, she will get a confidence boost. She thinks you are bragging about her cooking at work. This is adding to her RMV in her mind on a public level. You just pulled off the rare win (staying on plan), win (passed a shit/comfort test), win (publicly raising her RMV).

Now that is out of the way and you are still with us, there Sally, let's get another truth that directly correlates to the fee fees. You are not responsible for the happiness of anyone, but your own.

That's right, you are not responsible to make your wife, kids, or strangers happy. For a husband or wife, you are responsible for creating an environment where happiness can be obtained by the other spouse, i.e., bring in enough money to have a comfortable home, or keep it tidy and clean enough to allow for the other to be capable of happiness and not having to pick up after everyone. It is not your job to cater to anyone or ensure they are in THEIR best state of mind. That is THEIR responsibility, and surely not yours.

Additionally, Boys, if you think that it is your responsibility to ensure your woman's sexual satisfaction, you are sorely mistaken. A woman's climax takes many factors to happen, most of which are mental. As stated above, her mental state is HER responsibility, and you have no control.

As parents, you are also not responsible to keep your kids happy and, most importantly, entertained. If you behave like it's your job to make sure little Billy and Jackie are moving from one activity to another for all their waking hours of every day, you are limiting their ability to develop to a functional level. This action will eventually hurt them as adults. You are also covertly communicating that they are the center of the universe, which is far worse if you don't want to create needy, demanding adults that will only add to society's problems (don't make future inmates).

As a man, you should never ask if your wife or girlfriend is happy. This act will tip the scales so far from the masculine (lowing your SMV) and show that you think her happiness is your responsibility. You might as well just hand her your balls while you ask because you just failed a shit test that you created for yourself. High-value women only want men who just "get it", men who know how to be men and treat a woman like a woman. She will never overtly tell you how she wants to be treated, you will have to observe her actions as compared to yours. Some women don't even know what they want, just decide and their actions will tell you if it was right or not. If what you are doing produces a reaction that is pleasing to you, then you should keep doing what you're doing.

All militaries around the world function in a similar manner. First, they train, then field evaluate, and finally, an after-action report is done to gauge the efficacy of the training and execution. You should follow the same model. Learn what to do, do it, and evaluate. Did it work? Yes, keep doing it, until it doesn't. Did it work? No, Learn more and repeat.

Key point is to understand that women respond to and give more covert communication, and men respond to and give more overt communication. You will know all you need to know by focusing on her actions and not her words. You should also be focusing on your actions, more on what you are doing for yourself and how she responds to the results. As well as how people in the wild are changing their responses to you.

Another important aspect of "just getting it", is not to make her the sole focus of your life. She wants a man who is out doing important shit in the universe, or on a mission and not following her around like a lost puppy. Find something that needs fixing and fix it, at least try to look busy with something other than her.

For Christ's sake, once you fix something, don't run your mouth about it, just let her notice. If she doesn't notice, check your fee fees, you are searching for validation. If you chase her down and tell her that you fixed the leaky faucet, you are covertly projecting a little toddler who wants to hang his picture on the fridge. Just in case you were wondering, she is not going to drop her panties at your crappy-colored picture.

For the love of all things holy, you better notice and thank her for doing something for you. She needs validation, that's just how it is. If you question this, just look at Instagram and all the women showing their asses just for likes. A woman needs validation, and because of this, a man doesn't. A high-value man does something because it needed to be done, not for the parade afterward.

If you ask her if she is happy, you are covertly telling her that you revolve around her. This is a little bit more of that social conditioning, "happy wife, happy life" which is utter nonsense. If women communicated overtly then they would correct this falsehood. The covert communication that this is not working is the sky-high divorce rate in the western world.

GOOD COP BAD COP

"But if no one cares about my feelings, what do they care about?"

Outcomes and Impacts, that's it.

The world and everyone in it only give fucks about the outcomes and impacts of your actions. You can slave away for 12 hours a day at your job, but you only make $10 an hour, it doesn't mean much. That means your broke ass is only worth $120 a day.

There are positive and negative outcomes based on your actions. You could spend four years in college or got to a trade school. Both end with you walking out and starting a career. Both have good outcomes.

The impacts are the most important part of that equation. If you go to college to get a degree and rack up on average $27,000 in student loan debt. Then you start your career making on average $29,000. You won't be out of the hole until December of your first year of work, with no living expenses mind you.

If instead of going to college on your dime, you join the military and use the GI Bill while you are enlisted for your education. You leave the military with a trade, and an education and they paid you for doing it. The money that you would start making in your new career will be all yours from the first hour. That is a much better impact for the same outcome.

Another example is if you are 5'7" and put on 20 pounds, and your friend is 6'4" and puts the same amount of weight. That extra 20 weight is going to have a higher impact on you than on him. But, if you both lose the extra weight, it will have a higher impact on you then on him.

The point is the impact is individually weighted on the environment and situation. You may get to go balls deep in a coed, but your soon-to-be ex-wife is going to make your ass bleed in court. Understanding is key when you start running your plan, as you gain experience you should reevaluate your plan to ensure the goals are having a large enough impact. If you have a shit ton of work to do, you may need to start with a low-impact winning outcome to get the momentum to handle the larger shit.

Just in case you are not fast enough to get it, women will give a man anything he wants if he can get high impactful outcomes. The outcomes and impacts of your actions are a direct reflection of your masculinity and leadership SMV.

Money is a physical reflection of value. If you are making $10 an hour, you have less value then the CEO of the company you work for. This reflects his impact on the big picture as compared to yours. He probably has better sex with hotter women than you do too. Instead of getting hurt about it, and wasting time camping out on wall street, get your shit together, learn something, execute, and start banging swimsuit models.

The world does not care that you feel it's not fair.

Rules were put forth by Charles Sykes in his book "Dumbing Down America". Published 1996. It is good enough for Bill Gates to rip it off in 2000. We changed them to assist not pacify you.

Rule No. 1: Life is not fair. Get used to it. The average teen-ager uses the phrase "It's not fair" 8.6 times a day. You got it from your parents, who said it so often you decided they must be the most idealistic generation ever. When they started hearing it from their kids, they realized Rule No. 1.

Rule No. 2: Develop your self-esteem and your children will follow in your footsteps. The real world won't care as much about your self-esteem. Usually, when inflated self-esteem meets reality, kids complain that it's not fair. (See Rule No. 1) Some of the best advice I have ever been given on raising a child. Never worry about the direct threat to your child. Worry about the indirect threat. Teach and build their self-esteem! Build It from a moral and ethical compass. Let them fail, come in last, and get that frustrating feeling. This is called progress. Every negative element in life relies on the exploitation of a person's low self-esteem.

Teach them the difference between being hurt and being injured. Being hurt is a feeling and can be easy to overcome with the right guidance. An injury involves broken bones, open wounds, and torn muscles. Being hurt requires resilience, being injured requires a medical professional. The ability to identify this can save their lives one day.

Rule No. 3: Know yourself and seek self-improvement. It takes time and hard work. Things are not going to happen overnight. Journeys take time. You need to find what your gift is, find what you're good at, and dive headfirst into it. It will be hard; you will fail several times. Learn and grow from it! It's not your parents' fault. If you screw up, you are responsible. This is the flip side of "It's my life," "You're not the boss of me," and other eloquent proclamations of your generation. When you turn 18, it's on your dime. Don't whine about it, go out and improve your situation. Simply work harder than everyone else!

Rule No. 4: No job is beneath your opportunity to learn how to run a business. Flipping burgers is not beneath your dignity. Your grandparents had a different word for burger flipping. They called it opportunity. They weren't embarrassed making minimum wage either. With every job you have comes an opportunity to learn that business and then create your own from the knowledge you take away from it. Selling hamburgers or coffee is a highly profitable business. The trick is, don't stay an employee for too long. Also, don't run your new business with an employee mindset.

Rule No. 5: Failure is a gift of growth that's wrapped in frustration. Note, if you find yourself not frustrated by failure, you're doing the wrong thing.

Rule No. 6: Winning and losing are valuable lessons. Your school may have done away with winners and losers. Life hasn't. In some schools, they'll give you as many times as you want to get the right answer. Failing grades have been abolished and class valedictorians scrapped, lest anyone's feelings are hurt. An effort is as important as results. This, of course, bears not the slightest resemblance to anything in real life. (See Rule No. 1, Rule No. 2, and Rule No. 4.)

Rule No. 7: Don't compare your reality to anyone or anything. Television is not real life. Your life is not a sitcom. Your problems will not all be solved in 30 minutes, minus time for commercials. In real life, people have to leave the coffee shop to go to jobs. Your friends will not be as perky or pliable as Jennifer Aniston.

Rule No. 8: Be kind, humble, be honest, however never

for a second let someone take your dignity. Stand up for yourself and for what is right.

Rule No. 9: Never be afraid to start over again. Everything and everyone in life changes over time. Be flexible and stay positive.

Rule No. 10: Never work so hard making a living you don't have time to enjoy your life. Sure, parents are a pain, the school's a bother, and life is depressing. But someday you'll realize how wonderful it was to be a kid. Maybe you should start now. You're welcome."

Rule No. 11: Keep your dreams, your goals, and your love life to yourself. People will try to destroy things they're incapable of obtaining or understanding.

The below exchange was dramatized in the movie Blackhawk Down. It is unknown if the words were spoken or not, it doesn't matter. It is a perfect demonstration of men living their purpose and getting the job done, knowing it will cost their lives. If not them, then who?

"SFC. Shughart: [on radio] C-2, we're at the Six-Four crash site. Securing a perimeter. [to Durant] You all right?

CWO Durant: Yeah, I'm good.

Shughart: [handing him a weapon] You're locked and loaded. Any Skinnies come around these corners, you watch our backs. [He turns and starts outside]

Durant: Hey - where's the rescue squad?

Shughart: We're it. [exits]"

The words may not be real, but the actions were. MSG Gordon and SFC Shughart set a perimeter around a downed helicopter in the Battle of Mogadishu. They are credited with at least 25 dead and many more severely wounded enemies. They eventually were outmanned having depleted most of their ammo.

The enemy was able to overpower them, and they died defending a crash site and downed pilot, CWO Durant. Durant was eventually captured and held as a POW. He was later released by the Somali Militia. For their actions, MSG Gordan and SFC Shughart received the Medal of Honor posthumously.

Be like them. Know the risks and get it done anyway because it needs to get done. Men do things that need to get done. Shut your mouth, stop your bitching, no one is coming to help. Your it. You are the rescue squad.

In the coming chapters, we will cover the things that most men and women are vetting for in the dating process so that you can understand what evolution and biology have stamped into our DNA as a mammal that walks on two legs and how biology, environment, and society has molded men's and women's preferences.

THE RELATIONSHIP FRAMEWORK

"Women want the most Alpha male out of the 50 men they know, and men want the hottest woman he can tolerate."

- Stefan Aarnio

The natural relationship framework that has worked for millennia has been male and female, so that is what we have set as the example. It has also been traditionally a male-dominant and female-submissive form of relationship that has been the most successful throughout history. There may be some traits that will be demonstrated by both sexes. For example, a wife may be in a leadership role at work but can be submissive to her husband at home, and that does not diminish her accomplishment at work.

Here is a shocker, most women have no issue submitting to their husbands, only if he is of high enough value. Most men have a hard time understanding that women can seamlessly change between roles on a dime.

The key for the male in the relationship is to earn the female's submission. For hundreds of thousands of years, it was as simple as being the better hunter, or the most masculine, or the most protective in a ten-mile radius. Now, with modern technology and society, you must always be at the top of your game and represent the highest value you can, regardless of the situation or environment. You must bring your top-shelf stuff if you are trolling local watering holes for a one-night stand, running day-to-day errands (you never know who you might run into), going to a family dinner out, or if you have been married for 25 years.

Women have always practiced hypergamy, which is the unconscious desire to get the best man her value can reel in. This is the best way to ensure the genetic selection has been engrained into her DNA, just as you have been programmed to shove your seed in every hole that will lay still long enough, it is what it is, no point in getting pissy over it. You should have recognized it in high school.

The head cheerleader, the highest value female in the group, and the quarterback, the highest value male in the group always seemed to date no matter what high school across all western society. It is so prominent that most media that takes place in that environment follow this theme. The reason is that the cheerleader had the highest SMV (Sexual Market Value) of the females and the quarterback had the highest SMV of the males.

The relationship was most often an on-again, off-again drama discussed by more than just their inner circle. This is due to neither of them having a high

RMV (Relationship Market Value), and they saw no need to work on it as they were going to ride out life on their looks alone as it has been working for them for at least seventeen years. If not checked, the quarterback will continue to be a complete douche until his first divorce (when his ex-wife will knock him down a few pegs), and the cheerleader will still be a Cee U Next Tuesday and will one day grow into a Karen that demands unreasonable shit from store managers. To understand the Karen epidemic, Karen was probably a high-value young woman who pulled in a high-value man based on looks, and the idiot married her before the honeymoon phase of the dating phase was over (before the true personality came out). It's too late to divorce her because he knows that she will divorce rape him for more than half his shit and has just stopped giving a fuck enough to pass her shit tests and maintain his boundaries, so he becomes as unnoticeable as possible until he gets laid in the ground.

To understand the Relationship Framework, it is easier to visualize it like the following:

Male Aspects	Female Aspects
SMV	SMV
• Masculinity	• Femininity
• Attraction	• Attraction
• Leadership	• Agreeableness
RMV	RMV
• Protect	• Manage
• Provide	• Multiply
• Preside	• Motivate

SMV is always in play for both sexes, from as soon as eyes are laid on the other person. It is the initial attraction and the continued sexual desire. SMV is most known as the Hot Rating Scale, the favorite number of 1 to 10 to rate the attractiveness of the opposite sex.

RMV comes into play when either person is in search of a longer-term relationship than just a quick sexual romp. This will come into play for the best possible partner to mate with and form a relationship long enough and the ease of it to create offspring.

Relationship Ranks

As a man, it is imperative not to just promote women without a clear definition of titles. A promotion also comes with higher responsibilities and benefits, don't just hand that shit out for free to any woman showing some skin and gives you some attention.

Most interactions start with the initial contact. Your SMV is on high display at this moment. Your goal is to Initiate, Isolate, and Escalate (IIE) if your goal is to continue the interaction. The IIE model can be used with any contact regardless of the intended end state.

You as a man will always have to Initiate contact with a high-value woman. This is engrained in our DNA as a species. Women have always been on the receiving end of male attention. She has practiced the boundaries of shielding herself from constant male attention all her life. Men play offense, women play defense. You are not so special that she will switch sides.

Once you make that initial contact and start to build rapport and the chemicals are starting to react. You must Isolate her from a group. You must recognize the social conditioning of the Anti-Slut Defense (ASD); she has been told by all the female figures in her life that being a slut is bad. You can't get her over this, don't even try. If you are attempting to make her eyes roll to the back of her head, this is a key element.

There are some outliers that voyeurism is a major turn-on. Women who enjoy voyeurism are due to the fear of getting caught and the shame that can follow. For them the ASD is exciting, but use caution with this type of woman, as she may not make the best of mothers for your offspring.

Once you have her separated from her social network, you must initiate contact. Once initiating contact is accomplished, build rapport, separate her from outside influences, take the lead and be masculine. She has given you green light to this point. Be aggressive and attentive at the same time. Remember there is no such thing as movie-style lovemaking at first. It is all as rough as she will let you until she says stop. She will appreciate you and act better that way.

For the married man, if you are running your plan to get your SMV back up to acceptable levels, you will need to run some field tests to gauge results. Don't take any field tests past the Initiate phase. Once you separated another woman, you are putting yourself in a lose-lose situation. You will either cheat, or you have manipulated the other woman.

You need to get feedback from other women as your wife will give you tainted data and skew a representation of true progress. There is nothing morally wrong with two adults having a mutual conversation. The line is crossed once an action is taken to turn the conversation into a physical relationship.

The IIE model is also key. Your wife still has ASD, so you will have to work around that by isolating yourself. Then you must throw some masculine dominance her way by escalating.

We define Single as anyone not having a woman in the Girlfriend rank (covered in detail later). If you are single, you have a moral green light to run some game on any woman that you please. Understand that women do not play by the same relationship ranks as men, the lines are blurry due to hypergamy. They are driven to get the highest value man that they can, regardless of their status to you.

For a single man hit with the "I have a Boyfriend" line, all you have to do is respond with "Ok, I'm not the jealous type". She will be shocked at first, but hypergamy will overpower her outrage. If you have a higher SMV and RMV than a said boyfriend or if he is imaginary, you are in, my friend.

Understanding that women initially date men who are of higher value and status then they are. For example, a waitress is not going to date the bus boy, she is going to date the manager. She may bang the bus boy in the cooler, but her husband, he is never going to be. If you are attempting to date that hot nurse, you better make more money as a stock trader or just become a doctor. You may not have to go to such a great extreme if you have a shit load of status in other areas.

If you have a woman in the Girlfriend, Fiancé, or Wifey ranks, hypergamy is the reason to religiously run your plan and push that SMV and RMV as high as your genetics will allow. This is also a good reason to adhere to the vetting process and ensure that she is responding well to your progress on the plan.

Most men just blindly move through relationships and wake up one morning to a toddler banging pots in a pair of pull-ups, while his full-length bathrobe-wearing wife with a baby on her hip scrabbles some eggs. He looks down and can't even remember the last time he saw his dick without the assistance of a mirror.

This is usually when he decides to keep doing what he's doing and that his happiness doesn't matter. He will just get up every day and keep doing the same mediocre shit that got him there until his heart finally explodes.

Little does he realize that his wife and kids are not happy either. If he is lucky, she won't just pop smoke and file for divorce, instead, she'll just get her shit together. When that happens, she will start having sex with Chad McHorsecock, Mike Massiveloads, and Jimmy Assblaster who will happily fill the "voids" in her sexual life.

In case you did not realize this, Dating is the Vetting process. You better believe she is vetting you; you better be vetting her. Once she starts showing traits that earn a promotion then promote, if she starts showing traits that deserve demotion, then demote, after she can't or won't correct the behavior.

<u>Ranks</u>

A rank structure is a key to understanding the control a man possesses in the relationship framework. An easy one to remember is:

1. Fuck Buddy

This is a woman who has a decent enough SMV that you throw some vitamin D her way. She does not have the RMV high enough to promote to a higher rank. Something to have some sexual fun with, but not one that you can stand long enough to have dinner with. She will probably get nothing more than a cup of coffee from you post sexual release as a reward for her willingness.

2. Plate

This is a term from the Pick-Up Artists (PUA), it references spinning multiple plates from long sticks witnessed in talent shows. This is a woman who you are not exclusively dating. She has demonstrated a high level of SMV and has started showing some RMV. This is the first level of the relationship rank. You are dipping your toe at this end of the pool. You can still get out without much recourse. Just go find another plate. You can date multiple plates at the same time, just tell them about it. They will apricate the honesty and this will also promote healthy competition and overall, a higher SMV/RMV profile for all suiters.

3. Girlfriend

You have now promoted her high enough to drop all the other plates and date her exclusively. She has a high enough SMV and has demonstrated a high enough RMV to earn a little more benefit. This stage should last through the honeymoon phase (usually 18-24 months). During the honeymoon phase, you will not see her true long-term personality as both of your hormones are still kicked into high gear. Your hormones will start to level out in about two years. A woman at this rank can have some bad days, we are human after all, but she should be responsive to your leadership.

There is no need to move her in yet. It can work if you move her in at this stage, but you are betting the farm depending on your state's common law marriage laws. A breakup at this stage could be exponentially more troublesome if she is living with you. Be suspicious of any woman who is attempting to move in slowly by leaving things and reasoning that it's just easier that way. Maintain your boundaries in this stage, as it sets the tone for future promotions.

4. Fiancé

This is the last stage of vetting. The girlfriend has lasted the 24 months of your take no shit attitude and she is thriving. Both your SMV and RMV have been improving over the last two years and she is motivating you to continue your path. She has demonstrated that she is willing to submit to you for the long term. This is your last chance to demote without getting lawyers involved.

5. Wifey

The pinnacle of SMV and RMV, she is now tenured. If your dumb ass followed the rank structure and vetted her properly, you will have a happy life. If you didn't take the time or spend the energy, she now owns you, your kids, and at least half your shit. You will probably be paying her for at least the next 18 years, if not for her lifetime. Choose wisely.

Most women will start as a plate, as she has already demonstrated a high enough SMV that you are willing to completely bypass the Fuck Buddy stage and start researching her RMV. We suggest that any woman you are attracted to enter your life as a plate. Fuck Buddy status is reserved for demotion only. You have sexual chemistry with her, but your personality and/or values just do not align making her insufferable to be around.

Your requirements for promotion are individual, what is good for the goose is not always good for the gander. Your path may require a specific type of woman, your brother is on a different path that has different needs of support.

You cannot just meander through these promotions. You cannot succumb to the "What are we?" talk. Note this usually means the plate is ready to be dropped or promoted. You must decide. Remember if she is promoted, all other existing plates need to be reappraised for RMV before they all are dropped.

This is the strongest boundary that you must maintain. If you fail, you are projecting the weakest level of protection to the most important boundary of all. You can go ahead a kiss your balls goodbye, you are now a eunuch. You will never get submission from her. Anytime you attempt to demonstrate masculinity, she will shit test you until you cave. And, make no mistake, you will cave.

It is of utmost importance for a happy long-lasting relationship, once a promotion is given you do not remove the benefits from the previous rank, you just add more. If you received a promotion at work and they gave you a raise and dental coverage but removed your medical coverage, you would either not accept the promotion or find a new employer who didn't pull such bullshit.

For example, you will sometimes have to ravage your wife like a Fuck Buddy because you both need this from time to time. Remember your wife wants you to treat her like a girlfriend and wine and dine her ass like you used to.

Most marriages that are sexless, unhappy, or just going through the motions are due to the man removing benefits from the lower ranks. Usually, this happens unwittingly, just by getting too comfortable and having a false idea that "you have made it".

There is no such thing as making it, the only finish line is the grave. You can rest when you're dead.

The following has been circulating the internet for years.

Title: What should I do to marry a rich guy?

I'm going, to be honest about what I'm going to say here.

I'm 25 this year. I'm very pretty, have style and good taste. I wish to marry a guy with a $500k annual salary or above. You might say that I'm greedy, but an annual salary of $1M is considered only middle class in New York. My requirement is not high. Is there anyone in this forum who has an income of $500k annual salary? Are you all married?

I wanted to ask: what should I do to marry rich people like you?

Among those I've dated, the richest is $250k annual income, and it seems this is my upper limit. If someone is going to move into a high-cost residential area on the west of New York City Garden(?), a $250k annual income is not enough.

I'm here humbly to ask a few questions:

1) Where do most rich bachelors hang out? (Please list down the names and addresses of bars, restaurants, and gyms)

2) Which age group should I target?

2) Which age group should I target?

3) Why most wives of the riches are only average-looking? I've met a few girls who don't have looks and are not interesting, but they can marry rich guys.

4) How do you decide who can be your wife, and who can only be your girlfriend? (My target now is to get married)

Ms. Pretty

A philosophical reply from the CEO of J.P. Morgan:

Dear Ms. Pretty,

I have read your post with great interest. Guess there are lots of girls out there who have similar questions like yours. Please allow me to analyze your situation as a professional investor. My annual income is more than $500k, which meets your requirement, so I hope everyone believes that I'm not wasting time here.

From the standpoint of a businessperson, it is a bad decision to marry you. The answer is very simple, so let me explain. Put the details aside, what you're trying to do is an exchange of "beauty" and "money": Person A provides beauty, and Person B pays for it, fair and square. However, there's a deadly problem here, your beauty will fade, but my money will not be gone without any good reason. The fact is, my income might increase from year to year, but you can't be prettier year after year.

Hence from the viewpoint of economics, I am an appreciation asset, and you are a depreciation asset. It's not just normal depreciation, but exponential depreciation. If that is your only asset, your value will be much worse 10 years later. By the terms we use on Wall

Street, every trading has a position, dating with you is also a "trading position".

If the trade value dropped, we will sell it and it is not a good idea to keep it for the long term - the same goes for the marriage that you wanted. It might be cruel to say this, but to make a wiser decision any assets with great depreciation value will be sold or "leased". Anyone with over $500k annual income is not a fool; we would only date you but will not marry you. I would advise that you forget to look for any clues to marrying a rich guy. And by the way, you could make yourself become a rich person with a $500k annual income. This has a better chance than finding a rich fool.

Hope this reply helps.

signed,

J.P. Morgan CEO"

The above exchange was reported to have taken place on Craig's List in approximately 2010. It is most likely a hoax, but the simple fact that it is still alive and well should tell you all you need to know. Regardless of if the exchange took place or not is of no consequence to the reality of what the message is. Whoever wrote this is a genius due to the view that is taken when it comes to relationships. If you are a high-value man, you better vet that hot piece of ass for more then just the superficial. More on this in the coming chapters.

Always remember, you attract what you deserve.

<u>Dating Red Flags</u>

It is ill-advised to date a woman who is still married,

separated, in an open relationship, or the divorce papers are not finalized. Do not be a White Knight, dragons do not need to be slain and damsels do not need to be saved anymore.

Let her deal with the consequences of her decisions without dragging you down with her and wasting your resources to pay off her debt.

If she is a single mom and is not willing to introduce her kids to you in a reasonable amount of time, then she may not be a single mom. If she is attempting to bring you into her kids' lives sooner than you want, then she is attempting to throw you in the daddy role or she is hoping you get attached to the kids and overlook her issues. This will make you hesitate when you want or should leave.

If she came from an abusive relationship, had toxic partners in the past, or an active protective order, you need to tread lightly. There are going to be some trauma issues that come with these types of relationships. Most require counseling to overcome. Watch behavior carefully, and decide accordingly, do not stay in a relationship for the sake of a relationship. If you are not receiving the same level of benefit that you are providing, then leave it, you are wasting your valuable time, attention and resources.

If she is looking for work, on a temporary visa, or currently in counseling. She must be self-sustaining in her process of growth. She has her apartment at the very least. Any form of emotional insecurity in the first 90 days is an instant reduction back down to a buddy at best.

David makes good money in a coveted profession and has

a teenage child. He consistently gets involved with low value women who won't do the work to raise their value. He continuously dates woman who is out of work, going through a divorce, or has a bright future in the fast-food industry.

He is a college-educated professional who is extremely driven and is caught in a rotating cycle of failed relationships. All of this by his own selection process and inability to maintain his boundaries.

Yes, there is the occasion when the growth potential is very high in both of you and you're both going through a rough time. This is acceptable growth potential, and her character is the thing your big head should listen to.

The problem more so now than ever, is that you are weak, lonely, babied by your mother or female relative that raised you, and you will stay with almost anyone who will have sex with you and act as if they care. The definition of insanity...

Look it up and stop expecting and accepting the same results. Stop conducting yourself in the same way as you have in the past. You're here because it hasn't worked yet, so stop. Educate yourself and make a dating plan. Stay in your growth potential lanes. If she isn't willing to support you, then she stays a buddy or a plate.

MALE SEXUAL MARKET VALUE

"I'm too sexy for my shirt

Too sexy for my shirt

So sexy it hurts"

- Right Said Fred

To ensure a complete understanding of the framework as it has probably controlled your life since puberty and will continue to do so until you take your last breath, we will break down each individually.

SMV is what pulls people to each other and can extend the interaction to work toward promotions in the framework. If your SMV is high enough, this promotion process can be quite easy in the early stages. In the later stages, RMV has a higher value in the later stages of the relationship.

The key to a happy long-term relationship is to maintain, then maximize your SMV and RMV. They are the strong powerful defenders of your boundaries and standards. In the later stages, especially in a marriage, it is extremely important to not get completely comfortable. A little comfort is fine, marriage should be a relatively safe environment. However, always remember, you need a strong powerful SMV/RMV balance to keep outside influences at bay.

Understand how all of this plays a role in your relationship or it will be doomed to failure. The higher the level of relationship, the harder the fall. The woman you married is never the same one you divorce.

<u>Male SMV Masculinity</u>

Masculinity is based on society, in the US and Canada, it is more of a larger framed male, epitomized by football or hockey players. In Europe, it may seem a little more feminine than the US version, more of a soccer player or cyclist. It can best be characterized as dominance; some would describe it as Alpha traits and behavior.

The best way to exemplify masculinity is to stay on your plan or path of continual growth. Hobbies are a great way to demonstrate masculinity, things as sports, cars, and extra points for combat sports (boxing, MMA, kick boxing, etc.). Even more, points out if you are in a career that displays masculine power such as the military, law enforcement, or firefighting. Women get weak in the knees for a man in uniform or a well-tailored suit. How you dress plays a role in how you feel and the result of this determines how you are perceived by others. You can also add some masculinity by being a leader of other men, not just managing them, but leading them.

You can see that a high school quarter back is checking multiple boxes in this aspect; larger framed, striving for improvement through practice, football is a combat sport, uniform, and a leader of other men. You should be able to see that the captain of the debate team (talking is a feminine display) didn't stand a chance with the head cheerleader.

Masculinity is also displayed as silent dominance within a space. If you must tell anyone that you are dominate, you are not. Silent dominance is a display that enforces reasonable boundaries. Simple to say, but hard to do for most men due to the social conditioning that we have lived through, just stand up for yourself and stop being the nice guy. The world does not care about feelings, so why should you? You project this daily. The second a man meets this unspoken assessment of silent dominance he immediately elevated.

Sitting down at a card table for the first time with men you haven't met. This silence dominates in its rawest form. How you greet all of them, how you sit, your tone of speech, eye contact, and the way you move the deck or touch your cards. Also, how you bet, size, timing, eye contact or none, and how you move before and after the bet is made will factor in on the physical and mental response of the person and action you wish to influence.

You must remember all the equated movements and speech for every shown hand and never show your hand if you don't have to. A quality player will pick up on your pre-flop actions for every shown hand, and so will a woman. This is the essence of silent dominance. However, your position and chip count in which you started before the initial action being taken is important as well.

If you have ever noticed when a highly dominant man walks into a room and everyone stops to see what he does, that is the epitome of quiet dominance. Everyone just stops and pays attention, because of the way he is dressed, the way he carries himself, and his mannerisms. You can also rest assured that every woman in the room has noticed as well. She can't control it, it's in her DNA. Do the work and be that dude.

Communication is also a representation of masculinity, if you like to talk issues out constantly, especially, when a reasonable boundary has been crossed, you are failing in the masculinity department. Men do, they don't talk about it all day. You don't need to chew someone's ass out as punishment for a mistake, just remove yourself or your support. The time and attention of a high-value man is the reward for good behavior, he is always doing something to increase his gravitational pull, to get him to stop must be for something special. The punishment for a broken boundary is the high-value man's lack of time and attention. He will point out the error, usually with a single sentence, and remove himself until the person corrects it and starts respecting the boundary again.

Understand that the communication is not a display of dominance, the length (being short and to the point, to include a firm tone) is a slight display, but the walking away is the overall display of masculine dominance.

That is the key to getting corrective action from a woman, as she understands covert communication much easier and deeper than overt. The way this works is that the high-value man sees his time as a commodity. He is always demonstrating he is working on something or is busy with important shit. For this to work for you, you must Always Be Busy (ABB) working on raising your SMV or RMV. That way every second you spent giving her attention is a gift that she has earned.

the demographics of the conversation for the remainder of our flight. I asked, "what do you enjoy doing with the least amount of effort that creates the most positive and creative results for you"? He stated he is in the fire alarm system installation business, and it is probably putting the fire alarm systems. He was very proud of his seven years of experience and knew a great deal about the industry. I said great, now may I give you a personal challenge? He said yes. I asked him to at first spend an equal amount of time per day on learning what it will take to start and run a business of his own in the vocational skillset he is already in. He acknowledged my idea at this point and started to listen more attentively to the conversation. The iPhone went away, and I finally had his full attention. We chitchatted for a while about beginning a small business.

I asked if I could ask him another question, and he in turn agreed more willingly at this point. I enquired about his girlfriend or spouse. He stated they had recently broken up and wished they hadn't. I asked one simple question, the one I had to take 45 minutes to get to. Did her leaving you to have anything to do with your time playing video games? His face went blank and then he was amazed at how I knew that. He stated she was continually approached by his ex-girlfriend for over a year to stop playing so much.

I quickly pointed out it wasn't the game, or the time spent playing it, it was the overall time wasted. The fact he displayed a poor GPF, and she saw the future sitting there being wasted on fruitless games. He was astounded by the insight I had into his relationship he wanted to discuss it further. Instead, I focused on the importance of

47

Another important aspect of communication is not just what you say (content), or how you say it (tone), but also what tools you use to communicate. If you are having hour-long conversations on the phone with a woman, you are projecting feminine energy, she will see you as her best friend because you are acting like a teenage girl.

Phones, and to be clear, any apps (text messages, Facebook, Instagram, Tinder, them DMs, etc.) you use to communicate, should only be used to communicate logistics. The phone is only used to set up face-to-face meetings and coordinate those meetings. Keep all communication as short and sweet as possible. This is simply texting:

"I want YOUR spaghetti tonight"

"Be ready by six, wear the red dress I like"

And the best one of all is "Stockings, Heels, Nothing Else. I will be there in one hour."

You know you have made a dent in her psyche when you get a response of "Yes, Sir!" not just a fucking thumbs up emoji. Fair warning, you better have a plan when you get there, while she is standing in front of you in exactly what you told her to wear. A plan that should encompass all the activity that will be taking place while you make the beast of two backs, including how many orgasms you are going to give her and how we are going to get cleaned up after. This shouldn't be hard for you as you probably have been fantasizing about getting her that way, just play out the fantasy. Bonus points for having a date planned out to reward her for following your direction and submitting to your dominance.

Here is another piece that you may not realize, she just didn't take her clothes off and take five minutes to do what you said. She used the entire hour to do her hair, make-up, take a shower, shave, and a litany of other things to please you. At least be smart enough to know what to do with it once you get it.

Another great function of modern technology is the voice recording feature in text messages. Not the voicemail or the talk-to-text function, but the actual voice recording sent as a text. This allows you to convey the tone that texts can get wrong. They also allow her to be more discreet if she is in a situation where your texts can trigger the Anti Slut Defense (which is the cause of covert communication).

You can also use the sexual dress order text to set and enforce standards (like enforcing boundaries, both exude masculine dominance). The best way to do this is to shorten the time you give her to get ready before you arrive. If you like a clean-shaven woman, then hitting her with a shortened prep time will ensure that she will maintain that standard in the off change that she gets a text similar in the future. Just be sure to blow her mind in the sack to positively reinforce the good keeping of your standards.

We know what you are thinking, "But isn't that chauvinistic? I could never do that", buckle up buttercup, we have news for you. The reason that 50 Shades of Grey was a bestseller and turned into a trilogy of movies that brought in a total of $1.3 Billion (yes, with a B) was because modern women are craving the masculine dominance of old. Yet another sign of women's covert communication skills at work, and here you are too fucking stupid to listen or draw a correlation.

Another covert communication that you completely missed, is the tv show Yellowstone. The fourth season of the show was the highest-rated show of the year with a total of 11 million viewers for the season finale alone. The show draws a large audience due to most male characters are written and performed in a very masculine way. They are masculinity on full display. The only exception to this is the character of Jaimie, he is a whiny little bitch who allows everyone to manipulate him. He is written in a way that all his actions appear to be done because he was told to do them. Once he does what he is told, he constantly over-emotes to the point of being a child. He is universally hated as a character, due to his annoyance, much like a popcorn kernel stuck in your teeth.

Women are no longer getting masculine energy from men in the world on a day-to-day basis, so they want to play it out with the special man, let that man be you and not Chad McHorsecock. Chad is a train engineer for the Get Your Woman Lines and his favorite route is the Pound Town Express.

Just man up.

Male SMV Attractiveness

Attractiveness is the most important aspect when it comes to the initial impression of others. It is the first thing they notice and if you can sustain a healthy-looking physique, you will be treated better by everyone in your sphere of influence and have an easier time extending that sphere. It also plays a role in the masculinity and leadership aspects as it immediately portrays a masculine appearance and the discipline necessary to maintain it, which is a key element of leadership.

The importance of a wider shoulder-to-hip ratio (AKA, the golden ratio) cannot be understated. Since the beginning of time, a shoulder-to-hip ratio of 1.62 has been the gold standard for female tingles. This can be understood that if your shoulders are not at that ratio, you have some work to do, and it is very simple to understand; pick up heavier shit and stop putting so much shit in your face.

Understanding is easy, doing it is the hard part. Be consistent and maintain a positive standard. Stop making excuses and just do it, remember no one gives a single fuck that you are tired, or your muscles hurt, or you don't feel comfortable at the gym. Here's some news for you, if you are doing it right, a workout is not supposed to be comfortable, no one else is comfortable either, just get it done and stop being a pussy.

You will be motivated in the beginning, and that is great, however it won't last. Motivation is fleeting in nature, it may only last for a couple of months at best. During this time, it is important to develop your self-discipline. The discipline will turn that motivation into habit. Self-discipline is the only way to get to your hardest of goals.

Lifting weights should be the most important aspect of your plan. No matter what is happening on a lift day, you need to always make it to the gym, nothing else is more important. The benefits make everything in life better, not only are you working for the golden ratio, but the mental and physical benefits will far outweigh the time that it takes to pick up heavy stuff and put it down.

If you need to pass through the anger phase. After all, you

have been shocked to your fragile core that your world view has been shattered because you did everything, they told you to do, and you are still treated like a piece of shit. Put the heaviest weights you can safely lift on a barbell and imagine picking it up off the bloody mutilated corpses of your enemies, while their blood drips from the plates and loud music that you can't understand the lyrics to blasts in your ears. That should help your mental health and keep those fee fees in check.

Focus on lifting in the gym. Where are all the women going, to the treadmills, stair climbers, and stationary bikes, are the men are clanging metal plates together?

The Gym is not a pickup spot, it is a workplace. Now sometimes, natural occurrences with women will arise, but that is not what you are there for. You don't need to be a total dick if a woman chats you up on the way in or out or asks for help, just don't let it get in the way of the work, and NEVER initiate a conversation with a woman at the gym.

The absolute best thing you can do is vet your gym properly. The best gyms for men killing to get their SMV up is one in a warehouse with no AC or Heat and not a single machine plugged into a power outlet. These gyms are filled with similar-minded men that intimidate women and weaker-minded boys; this will eliminate unneeded distractions. By distractions, we mean the half-naked women, who leave nothing to the imagination wearing booty shorts and a sports bra and taking selfies in the gym mirror for the gram. Then out you as a creeper for the slightest of glance in her general direction and the fall out of going viral.

You may also be intimidated by the environment, but rest assured this is the closest thing you can get to a Men's Club in modern society. The men in this type of gym will leave you alone as they are there to get shit done, the only exception to this is when they see you do something stupid that will cause injury. If you are busting your ass, they will even give you props as motivation to keep on your path.

If you can't find a gym like this in your area, then you can build one in your garage. All you need is a barbell, a squat rack, a bench, and plates, that's it.

That should be your Man Cave, you can even put up a "No Girls Allowed" sign for good measure. If you have a man cave in your house with nothing more than a tv and a lazy boy so that you can watch ESPN in peace, you are wasting valuable time and space.

Your woman is watching this, every minute you are sitting on your ass blankly staring at the tv, phone, or God forbid playing a fucking video game, your value is dropping.

SMV/RMV Growth Potential Factor, (GPF)

I met George on a plane to LA, he was in his early thirties, and we sat next to one another for approximately 30 minutes before I made initial contact with him. I had noticed he was single, well-mannered, and dressed in the typical SoCal style of clothing. I noticed he was playing GTA the entire time on the plane.

The conversation was light and humorous at first, then I asked him how long he plays a day. He replied around three hours or more. I asked one question that change his display of GPF in the future.

GPF also works for JMV as well. Always Be Busy (ABB) and always be on an educational and vocation growth plan. Lifelong learning. Continuously displaying growth in different aspects of the vocational field of expertise your in. There is one important factor involved in the GPF in relationships or on the job, Do Not Talk About It! Just quietly go about it and the results will be naturally manifested within the work or relationship you're in, stop looking for validation from others.

The point that took me an hour to get him to was this; I needed him to realize it was the lack of growth potential factor he was displaying each time he got on the game. It was taking away from time that he could have been reading, planning, educating himself and overall self-improvement. Time spent sharing his knowledge and the potential path he was on. He sat there in silence for the rest of the flight.

Take the game or whatever is diminishing your GPF outside and set it on fire, throw a gym in your garage, and if you must, watch ESPN while you pray at the Iron Church.

Keep good oral and overall physical hygiene, keep your hair and nails trimmed, and if you have one, your beard on point. Just lean into your genetics and shave your dome. There are plenty of men who shave their heads that get plenty of attention. Remember that you are responsible for your happiness and wellbeing.

For Christ's sake, stop dressing like a hobo. There is a reason when you buy jewelry from a reputable store, they put it in a velvet pillowy box and not just throw it in a brown paper bag. The packaging represents the value of the item inside. What is the point of sacrificing to the god of war in the Iron Church to get the golden ratio, then wrapping it in a crusty newspaper?

Be the best-dressed man in your environment. That does not mean you go black tie dress to the grocery store, but it doesn't mean go in your sweatpants either. This goes back to setting and maintaining standards. Even if you are doing something as mundane as grocery shopping with your wife, you can still spice the process up with a nicer tone of dress.

It's as easy as not going anywhere in public in anything less than a button-up short sleeve dress shirt. Wearing that to the gym is just asinine. The gym is work; a t-shirt is acceptable for any environment where physical work is being performed, but at least try to wear one without pit stains and holes in it, you're doing masculine manual labor, have a little pride in your work. Don't say a word either, just do it, throw some grunts in there for good measure.

An interesting thing starts to happen when you kick your dress game into high gear, you are setting a new standard, and the wife will follow suit. All women know and understand hypergamy, she does not want to trot alongside a husband or boyfriend dressed to the nines in her holey jeans, t-shirt, and Chuck Taylor All-Stars. At the least, she will throw a blouse on and pair the jeans with some heels as a warning to other women that she is the one riding your meat pole. You also get the pleasure of dragging a nice piece of ass around the grocery store as arm candy and the heels make her ass look fantastic when she needs something off the bottom shelf.

For a date night, you pull off a pair of nice blue jeans, a long sleeve dress shirt paired with a dress vest (vests can be sinched in the back for a tailored look to accentuate the golden ratio), and some exotic boots. She can complement this (as instructed, of course) in a skintight dress that matches the color of your vest, stockings, and heels, and nothing more. You both know what's going to happen after the formality of the date has concluded, no need to allow her to wear things that will get in the way.

Charisma is another aspect of the attractiveness trait that women are highly attuned to. You may look like a Greek god and dress like a cover model, but if you can't string words together to form a conversation then she is going to pass on any form of future with you.

People will volunteer information to you constantly. All you must do is listen and then ask for more based on what they provide. If someone gives you just a small amount of information, you can spin that into an hour-long conversation that no longer resembles the original content. However, only if you want it to, remember, time and attention are a commodity.

A key component of this is confidence. You need to act like you have been there and done that. Nothing is new to you, and nothing will surprise you. Just be confident and relaxed. This will allow you to be quick with your wit which will increase the display of confidence and charisma. A mindset that you are the prize (which you are or working to become), will help this aspect become easier to adjust to.

You can practice this in the field anytime you need to be able to recognize free information and ask follow-up questions to keep the conversation going. It can be anyone you please, the cashier at the gas station, the receptionist at the doctor's office, or the bank teller. Just do your best to keep a relevant conversation going and adjust the results.

Women love talking about themselves and if you can turn a half-hour coffee date into an hour and a half, you have succeeded in raising your attractiveness on her scorecard. Added points if you throw a few cocky and/or funny comments as a response to show that you have a funny bone. If you are in public with your woman, and she is witnessing a polite conversation with a stranger, she will enjoy watching your articulation and observation skills. If you are speaking to another woman and having a plutonic conversation, then you are covertly communicating to her that your relationship is secure. If the other woman is flirting but you are glossing right over the advances and pulling the other woman into your frame and controlling the conversation, this is even more effective with your wife.

Male SMV Leadership

Now we wrap the male sexual market value up in a leadership role. Leadership and dominance are similar, but not the same as you cannot dominate without leadership first. There are multiple books on leadership that you should be absorbing and putting into practice, so there is no reason to be long-winded here.

You need to understand how leadership plays a role in your relationship. Women do not, only under a very few exceptions, want to be the head of a household and make big decisions. A democracy cannot exist with only two people, someone must be solely responsible. They don't want the responsibility or accountability that comes with this position. That is why the Captain and First Officer model has worked for millennia.

The Captain (CPT) is the one and only person fully responsible person for the ENTIRETY of the relationship. The First Officer (FO) is there to assist with the day-to-day operations of the household to free up the CPT's time and energy to handle the big picture stuff like setting vision, mission, and goals.

She is also there to ensure that things are kept on track and that the CPT's standards are maintained when he is not present. The FO has the full authority of the CPT and at times she can have control of the ship, but the CPT has veto power.

Your leadership skills play a pivotal role in the Preside aspect of the RMV. She will be looking for this leadership during the dating phase to vet if you have the skills to Preside over the household in the later stages of the relationship.

Demonstrating leadership is simply having a plan and working on it. You need an overall plan, and then you can break that down into yearly, monthly, weekly, and daily plans.

It is also key to create a plan for dates in the early stages of the relationship and continue this practice for as long as it lasts, this will require you to plan almost down to the half-hour increment. You will also need to plan for any unforeseen circumstances that could arise and be ready to call an audible, if necessary. If the restaurant didn't honor your reservation because a tire runs flat, and it takes you 15 minutes to change it. You should know how to do it because it's masculine as hell. Women love to watch a man take charge and get shit done and move on without much fanfare. Are you going to chalk this up as a loss and drop her back off or are you going to adapt?

The easiest way to get and maintain a high level of leadership is to Own Your Shit. Then when you have vetted and promoted her to a higher relationship level, Own Her Shit. Then years down the road when all the crazy caveman sex produces offspring, Own Their Shit too. Just carry around a massive bag of shit and dispense guidance and enforce standards and boundaries, with enough work, the shit you must own will fit in a coin purse.

Male SMV Big Picture

All the Male SMV attributes blend amongst the others much like a Venn diagram. One will affect another and so on. You can have a high attractive and masculine scale and you will be nothing more than a "Fuck Boy", that may be great in your 20s, but it's going to suck when you get into your 30s and beyond. You may have a high leadership scale and be nothing more than a "Non-Gay Bestie", where is the fun in that?

The SMV also weights on the RMV aspects, so it is important to stive to be the total package and become a man who "just gets it". If you max out in one or two areas more than the other your relationship is going to be as wonky as a broken bicycle tire. The relationship is going to be much harder to get down the road. If it already is behaving badly, and there is no improvement then one of you may decide to ditch it. That is the easier of the options on the surface, but then you're left with walking the rest of the way when you could just fix the tire.

FEMALE SEXUAL MARKET VALUE

"Show me the woman he sleeps with, and I will tell you the projected value of himself. No matter what corruption he's taught himself about the virtue of selflessness, sex is the most profoundly selfish act of all acts, an act which he cannot perform for any motive but his enjoyment – just try to think of performing it in a spirit of selfless charity! – an act which is not possible in self-abasement, only in self-exaltation, only in the confidence of being desired and being worthy of desire. It is an act that forces him to stand naked in spirit, as well as in body, and to accept his real ego as, his standard of value.

He will be attracted to the woman who reflects his deepest vision of himself, the woman whose surrender permits him to experience – or to fake – a sense of self-esteem. The man who is proudly certain of his value will want the highest type of woman he can find, the woman he admires, the strongest, the hardest to conquer – because only the possession of a heroine will give him the sense of achievement, not the possession of a brainless slut."

- Ayn Rand

Females and Males of most species are different and

complimentary. Their traits have been passed down through generations to form a partnership to ensure the continuation of the species. As each generation creates more offspring, the selection process is programming the offspring for the best possible outcomes. Meaning, every generation is slowly growing better. The key point to this genetic improvement over time is the mate selection process.

In the current social society that we live in, women control the access to sex and men control the access to long-term relationships. Meaning the selection process is controlled by women in short-term sexual selection, but men control it in the long term. Both sexes are vetting for genetic supremacy for their offspring. Just with dread and hypergamy, you can get pissy if you want, but you can't change facts with fee fees.

Understanding the facts are key to having them work for you instead of against you. You read in the last chapter about how to develop yourself or select the best partner as it concerns men's SMV. Now we will concentrate on the time-tested best female SMV attributes to aspire to or search for.

Female SMV Femininity

Women need to feel wanted; men want to feel needed.

For a man, the true feminine form is the basis for most of our lives. A feminine form is a basis for an entire art form. Edmund Burke wrote in 1757 "Observe that part of a beautiful woman where she is perhaps the most beautiful, about the neck and breasts; the smoothness; the softness; the easy and insensible swell; the variety of the surface, which is never for the smallest space the same."

Men spend most of their lives attempting to be as close to the feminine form as possible, on some occasions they may be able to get inside her for a few minutes and get as close to heaven that any mortal can. The female form has been the downfall of many a great man, who did not possess the restraint to tell her no. The first and most famous one is Adam.

The true femininity of a woman is hard to pin down and what is feminine to some men does not hold the same weight to others. However, we will go over the most agreed-upon descriptions, if you cannot identify it as pleasing then just look for others in a potential mate.

The most modern "traditional" relationship standard was set in the 1940s and 50s. To most men and women, if they are being honest, that is the ideal marriage format and is still something to strive for. During this timeframe, women wore mainly dresses, stockings, and heels. A manner of dress so feminine that cross-dressing men use them as a go-to to transform into a feminine form today. If you want to know what feminine dress looks like, observe what cross-dressers are putting on.

If you are still questioning this statement, let's look at the traditional dress for a bride at her wedding. The most important thing the bride concerns herself with is what she wears down the aisle. Women may change their minds on the type of dress they finally land on, but rest assured, she has dreamt about the dress since she was young. With the right dress, a woman can finally fulfill the princess fantasy since she was a toddler playing dress-up.

In case you have not been to a traditional western wedding in a while, there is a ceremony at the reception in which the groom goes under the bride's dress. There are some variations to the manner, but it results in the same, the groom pulls the bride's garter from her holding her stockings up and throws it into a group of single men. The man who catches the garter is the one destined to marry the next.

The most sensual female form is an individual's preference of the bust/waist/hip ratio. High heels accentuate this ratio and can draw the male gaze to the legs and ass of a woman. Observed, but little acknowledged among women is that heels also provide an audible stimulus to an approaching feminine woman. For most men, the clank of heels will make him lose his train of thought for a second. Ladies, take note, do you want a little more male attention? Ditch the flip-flops and throw on a pair of heels.

To further the point, during the 40s and 50s, a new art form sprouted, the Pin Up. Yes, the art was mainly used for advertising, but you can't argue the effectiveness of most companies using the same type of advertising for over a decade and beyond.

The Pin Up is the epitome of the modern female form. The female form with the combination of the most accentuating manner of dress. The Pin Up art, due to being publicly consumed, must only hint at the sexual nature of the situation, and could not be overtly sexual. As such, the artists had to present the female form in the current fashion and sexualize it. They created situations that a woman would naturally be in and in their natural dress could be extremely sexually appealing.

They were masters of representing the female form with all its curves and able to exaggerate the bust/hip/ waist contradictions that occur in every healthy feminine woman.

The art form is still popular, and some women will get all dolled up and replicate the look as much as possible today. Covert communication in action.

Yes, we know, "but this is all about clothes, aren't y'all going to cover that in the attractiveness aspect.". Great job, there high speed. It will be covered again. We are covering it because of the importance that her level of the dress will add or subtract from her femininity. You also need to understand that her femininity can be multiplied by her putting some effort into it. However, you will see her in ways that will completely detract from it. Sweatpants and a baggy t-shirt don't hug the curves of her body in the least. Just know, that the curves that you are craving to wrap your arms around are still there.

Men's dress has little availability to hide their masculinity. No matter how baggy a man dresses, his shoulders and chest can still show a muscular form. Women, on the other hand, can hide their femininity. All they need to do is cover the ratio, and they have become a frumpy cat lady.

The reason the standard traditional dress is a form-fitting dress, stocking, and heels is that it forces the appearance of elegance. Never underestimate of power of a woman displaying elegance.

Elegance is the main power of the feminine. Most women have a natural walk that sways the hips. Throw some heels into the strut and it can be hypnotic. If you pair, it with a pleated dress to exaggerate the sway of the hips and men will drool at her presence.

All the dress material in this section is forcing and intended to bring attention to the elegance factor that the woman can present. Yes, the present is used on purpose. You will need to pull the elegance from her. You can do this easily by running a little game on your wife. You need to understand that puling this off to her standards, requires an abundancy of time and energy.

When she uses the energy to put herself together for you, you have better make a flattering comment (immediately), find every excuse to touch her, and you better make that pussy rain once you get her out of that dress. The elegance that a woman "naturally possesses" requires a tremendous amount of energy to pull off adequately. A high-value man will recognize the facts of her effort.

Feminine energy is also demonstrated by her nurturing ability. If men and women are complimentary, men are the nature aspect of life and women are the nurture. The yen and the yang of a relationship. This is engrained into her DNA. Historically, women are the majority caregiver to the offspring until they can transition to solid foods. Women's ability to nurture will have direct effects on their motivation to help raise their children. This has some RMV aspects as child rearing is a long-term aspect, but if she can't or won't help if you are temporarily incapacitated then see that as a sign of inability to properly raise a child.

Nurturing adds to the feminine mystique that a woman presents. It forms in her actions, how she treats people that are below her social status is a key indicator of her nurturing ability. If she treats service workers like medieval serfs at her beck and call, rest assured, that if your value lowers, she will treat you the same way.

How she treats animals is an excellent way to determine if she has a nurturing capability that meets your needs. Animals can have a similar status to a woman as a child. If she is not willing to help you with the work to properly care for a dog, then take that as a sign that you will be doing the heavy lifting with your kids.

Female SMV Attractiveness

The commonly desired female ratio of bust/waist/hip ratio is 36"-24"-36", so much so that songs have been written about it. The reason for this is the ideal masculine body is V tapered as a contrast to this is the hourglass figure of the feminine. It is so appealing that the sole reason for corsets is to force the figure when it cannot be obtained naturally.

Which, to be clear, a full foot difference in measurement is damn near impossible. Hence the need for the corset. Know that they are not very comfortable, so if she squeezes into one for you, she has plans and you better be ready to make it worth her trouble.

Men are driven to put a baby in every woman that will lay still long enough for him to drop some seed. To ensure the best outcomes for his offspring he will gravitate to women who represent those outcomes. Therefore exomorphic (tall, low body fat) men will be attracted to endomorphic (wider framed, higher body fat) women. This is to ensure a healthy "middle ground" for his offspring.

For most men, attractive women can be several different kinds of women. As women need to be impregnated by the highest value man, men need to impregnate the highest number of women. Because of this, men are not picky when it comes to female attractiveness.

The majority of what determines attractiveness in women is other women. The fashion industry and media play a large role in imprinting their definitions of what is attractive in women. Men, however, like whatever resembles traits that flipped the boner switch and got their hormones moving.

For the men, lust what you lust, you are the only one who must stick his dick in it. For the ladies, accept that your man lusts after you constantly, no need to go changing what he lusts after too drastically. That is if it is healthy, and he is not asking you to balloon to 350 pounds. There are plenty of 350-pound women out there that can scratch that itch.

Here is where the lines blur between femininity and attractiveness.

To a high-value man, femininity is attractive. She may have a few pounds to lose, it doesn't matter. If she has feminine elegance and grace, she can join him in his plan and his leadership will take care of it. High-value men have a way of making high-value women and vice versa.

For a high-value man, a feminine woman can become a highly attractive woman with little work. It is more important to him that she be feminine and submissive so that the growth process can take place. If she is refusing to follow his lead, then she will be nothing more than a short-term Fuck Buddy and never make a promotion. He will bore her and call it off.

Generally, feminine attractiveness is the opposite of masculine attractiveness. Long hair, manicured nails, and the hourglass figure are the obvious signs of feminine attractiveness. But there are so much more, including smaller stature, being soft-spoken, and displaying feminine mystique to a man's mystery.

A less drastic hourglass ratio can be amplified by a more feminine dress and grooming to overcome some short comings. The closer a woman can come to the Pin-Up ideal the more attention she will get from high-value men. This also shows a willingness to stand against a crowd wearing t-shirts, ripped jeans, and tennis shoes. The Pin-Up style of dress takes work, and it is a direct reflection of her give a shit.

A woman dressed in a feminine manner (to accentuate her feminine form) is a key indication that she has respect for herself, and she is in pursuit of a high-value man that can lead her to the highest level of her genetics.

<u>Female SMV Agreeableness</u>

Agreeableness is the precursor to Submission. If she can't take direction and argues every damn time you direct her to do something, especially if it is for her benefit, then you are going to be in for a bad time.

Agreeable behavior is key to the SMV of a woman. The RMV of a woman is dependent on her submission to male dominance. You can vet for this attribute by witnessing her behavior with and her ability to submit to her father.

The common saying "No matter how good-looking she is, someone is tired of her shit", sums up the importance of this trait.

A woman's agreeableness can be tested in the very early stages of the vetting process. It can be done by sending the "Be ready by 6, in the red dress" text. If any of the directions are not followed, i.e., she is not ready by 6, or in the red dress, her agreeableness is in question. She may have a good reason for not meeting all the directions; the red dress was at the cleaners, or a pipe burst in the bathroom that prevented her from hitting your time hack. Or you are a fucking idiot and underestimated the amount of time she needs to pull off the look you requested.

If the reason was not that you are a fucking idiot, the rest of the time you run this plan and you get the same negative result, then there is a bigger issue. If she can't be ready on time and in what you requested, then she is demonstrating that she can't manage her time.

You can give her one last chance depending on the length of the relationship or you can go straight to removing your time and attention.

This behavior can be categorized as a shit test. The only response to this is to do the plan without her. If she can't get ready in the reasonable amount of time that you gave her in the dress that you requested. Then go on the date stag. Leave her to watch Netflix in the dress you told her to wear.

If you are running your plan and getting positive high impact outcomes, then she understands that your time is important. If she leaves you waiting for longer than a five-minute window, then it is a failure on your part to maintain your boundaries. If you do nothing, then you are no longer in control of the frame and you are failing to lead the relationship.

Her level of agreeableness will have a direct effect on your ability to run your plan. Agreeableness is correlated to a woman's neediness. If she is not agreeable, then you will be spending most of your time attending to her "needs". She will also be a shrill woman who is going to constantly nag you to take care of things that she could easily do.

Keep in mind that you are the Captain of the relationship, your time is better spent working for the long-term goals of the family which should be incorporated into your plans. If she, has you chasing her Honey Do List, you can't focus on moving the relationship in the direction that it needs to go.

If you are at the Fiancé rank or below, now is the time to question a demotion. Of course, removing your time may solve this issue quickly. However, if she has been conditioned as a new-wave feminist, you are probably shit out of luck. She is going to push back against you, because the future is female, and she "doesn't need a man".

If this is the case, just demote and be clear about the reasons why. Her agenda is in direct conflict with your path, and you need someone who will support and not sabotage progress for the sole reason that you are a man and men are bad.

The reason she has a Honey Do List in the first place is that you are not performing your duties as the CPT. Get your shit together and do it before she asks. Or, even worse, she has unreasonable standards and you have failed too many shit tests. In this case, you aren't the CPT of shit, you're just swabbing the deck of her ship.

MALE RELATIONSHIP MARKET VALUE

The role of a man in a relationship is to Protect, Provide, and Preside over all people and things in the household. Women, regardless of what they say, long for the safety, security, and leadership that a high-value man provides. Almost all women will submit to a man with high enough SMV and RMV.

Set goals based on your purpose.

Be goal orientated; have a personal goal, relationship-based goal, job market goal, and financial goal. Formulate a plan and speak it into existence regularly. Create a vision board. Have this board on the daily site. Vision boards in the office or on top of the refrigerator. Place it in a key location where it's unavoidable to not see it.

Just having goals and working on them will bring value to the relationship. Make one of your goals to read at least one book a month and then after the first-year attempt to double that goal. The average American who reads consumes twelve books a year. Most people after high school don't read a single book.

The power of setting goals and working towards completion is the subconscious growth potential she needs for your relationship to grow. This alone could change your relationship for the better.

Women are genetically programed to submit to the highest value man that they can bring in. Social conditioning has spent years convincing her otherwise, to some degree of success. But, when a high-enough value man comes on the scene, she will happily kneel to him a let him shove his dick in her mouth.

Your plan should not only focus on raising the SMV traits but should also focus on the RMV traits. If you want any chance of a successful marriage, you must display a high-value Relationship Market Value during the vetting process.

<u>Male RMV Protection</u>

Men are physically larger and have more upper body strength than women. Understand that women and children expect a man to be able to protect them if the need arises. The need may arise at any time in any location. You need to be able to call upon some violence when it is needed to protect ALL women and children, not just your own.

Yes, getting your wife and children out of a dangerous situation is protecting them. However, a woman will see you as less of a man if you fail to do everything you can to protect all the people who cannot protect themselves in the area.

In all the history of the human species, men have been disposable. War is fought by men for a reason, a single man can repopulate an entire civilization with enough willing women. Through DNA testing, Genghis Khan is a distant father of 8% of the entire world's male population. Women are the prized sex of our species. You are required to act like it.

You can do several things to raise your ability to protect her and her offspring. You can train in combat sports, you can learn to effectively use firearms, and you can even install an alarm system if you are too much of a pussy to put a gun in your hand or get punched in the face. You should probably also change the batteries in the smoke detector instead of just pulling the dead battery out. Generally, earning enough money to safely place you and your family geographically speaking in an area with good schools and low crime rates are also prime examples of Male RMV.

The slightest thing you can do to raise your capacity for controlled violence, the more your woman will respect you. If you are raising your SMV and working on your ability to protect her through combat sports will have added benefits to your attractiveness.

There are slang terms for women who exclusively date military (Barracks Princess) and law enforcement (Badge Bunnies or Holster Humpers). They are attracted to these men's ability to protect them. The uniform also exudes masculinity for these men.

You will need to ask yourself if you are hesitant to learn these vital skills if you are uncomfortable due to a true reason, like a disability, or if is it the social conditioning or the intrusive laws in your environment. If it is because of a disability, then you may need to get somewhat creative. If it is because of the laws of your land, why are you still living in a place that does not regulate to the reality of the world?

If you refuse, thinking that it won't happen to us, you need to check your Safe World Theory. It will happen to you eventually as you are projecting to the world that you are a Victim. You must get out of your comfort zone and learn this shit; it could save your life one day. A large part of how you're treated in the real world, on the street is the persona you project when that element first sees you. Is he someone I can take advantage of; will he resist or fight back? In short, approximately 90% of this equation is communicated through covert, nonverbal actions. Having quality situational awareness, being in shape, direct eye contact when passing someone, and countless other traits that exuded confidence.

Don't participate in people's self-destructive habits or addictions. Anyone who has had an addict in their life can attest that they pull everyone else down with them. If you give them even an inch, they take a mile. Surely, that is not in your plan. You must cut people out of your life that does not provide you any value.

Most people have a hard time understanding the consequences of everyday action and the long-term effects. Once a child touches a hot stove, that consequence is engrained in the unconscious mind for all time. This is due to the immediate and harmful effects of their action.

Protecting people from their day-to-day bad decisions that lead to self-destructive behavior is a more challenging part of the protective traits. This aspect depends on the submission of the other person to be effective. If you have a teenager who has a hard time meeting curfew after repeated attempts to correct this behavior. It is time to remove your support for this continued self-destructive behavior.

You will need to take the car, cancel the insurance, and no longer provide money for fuel. Make sure that they check in periodically and when there is a location change. Set the burglar alarm at night to prevent them from sneaking out. They go into lock down. This may be the standard operating procedure until they prove to be trustworthy or leave the house for college.

Some people may see this as an overreaction to typical teenage rebellion, however, if you talk to anyone in the medical field (Doctors, Nurses, EMTs) or Law Enforcement or Fire Fighting, nothing good happens after midnight. You are protecting your rebellious teen from their self-destructive behavior.

This mindset of protection also applies to spouses. If you have a spouse who smokes, they should know the dangers of this habit. Yes, they are adults that can make their own decision. However, you will be the one taking care of them in the latter stages of life and the medical issues that arise from smoking will make your golden years more accurately your bronze years. Medical bills that are the result of a habit that could have been dealt with earlier in life can destroy your retirement plans.

You need to decide how much sacrifice you are willing to endure because your spouse couldn't stop smoking for 30 years. Even if you are not directly supporting the habit by funding it, you are indirectly supporting the habit by continuing to stay. You are providing an environment that is conducive to the continuation of the habit.

Do you want to be the asshole who leaves his wife while she suffers from lung cancer? Or are you willing to take the easier option and pull the trigger now while you still have an opportunity to rebuild your life after the initial aftermath of a divorce in your 40s? Or are you going to suffer the consequences of your wife's decisions and stick it out until you're a widower in your 60s?

The outcomes of your ability to protect your inner circle can have very long-lasting effects on your happiness much later in life. You need skills to protect your family and women will be vetting for this as soon as she decides that you are more than just a one-night stand.

<u>Male RMV Provide</u>

Since the beginning of time, men have been required to provide for their tribes and families. Men started as hunters providing much-needed protein and fat that did not naturally grow in the environment. It is believed that the human brain exists today due to the rich fats that were obtained through the act of hunting.

Later in the dawn of agriculture, men were still required to provide this skill as the manual labor for planting and harvesting crops was back-breaking work.

This work was better suited for men because of their naturally higher levels of strength. In the Industrial Age, men built and maintained the machinery needed to create the homes we live in and the skyscrapers that we work in. They built the factories that allowed the mass production of everything from toothpaste to cars and trucks. Men have built the modern world and maintain it to this day. If your lights come on when you flip the switch, thank an electrician.

All that you need can be obtained by a quick trip to the store or you can get it delivered tomorrow from

Amazon. The only requirement is to have enough money to purchase the items needed. This means the more digits you have in front of the decimal point in your bank account the better you can provide.

If it were only as easy as wiping out a bank statement to display this ability. To women, your ability to provide is more complicated (what isn't with them). They also look at your potential ability to provide. They do this by vetting your ambition and drive.

You can sit on the couch and want to make six figures (ambition), but if you don't have the will to get it (drive), or at least a way to find that will then your wants mean nothing. Shit in one hand and wish in the other, see which one fills faster. The vetting process for this is ongoing, even after you are married. Recall that the grave is the finish line.

Women will listen to what you say and watch what you do to determine if you have the ambition to live up to your drive and vice versa. If you tell her your dream is to own your own plumbing company. She will watch to see if you are making decisions and acting as if that is where your plan is taking you.

In the above scenario if you are not taking classes or getting an apprenticeship, instead you are screwing around on Xbox all day, then you are telling her loud and clear that you lack drive. She knows that she will most likely have to be the bread winner and hear from her mother how much of a bum you are. You had better hope that the pipe you are laying in the bedroom is enough of a benefit to keeping her around for the long haul.

Yes, you could inherit your father's plumbing business,

but if you can't expand it, then you are showing a lack of ambition and/or drive. Good enough, never is. You must always strive to improve over time. It is fine to have setbacks from time to time, the average is what matters.

The easiest way to understand this is a Baseball Player. If you see consistent improvement in the batting average over a career, even with some off seasons. Then the improving player can get better contracts than a consistently mediocre player. The outcome is that the player who improves will be able to provide better for his family than the mediocre player.

The lack of providing ability is the number one (outside of adultery) cause of divorce in the western world to date. This means, the less money you can bring in, the more likely you are to get a divorce.

Money is a direct reflection of the value that you bring to a company or marketplace. If you don't make enough money, then you must raise your value to the company or find a better product to sell.

Even more simplistically, money is a value of your ambition and drive. If you don't make enough, but through your ambition and drive, learn other skills that can help in your profession, then it should equate to a higher salary. If it doesn't, then you should be driven to find a place that will pay you for it.

The example of the plumber is good for this as well. The plumber attends a trade school, gets an apprenticeship, and works for a company for five years. He is now 25, he goes out on his own and for five more years he has a high enough client base he has hired ten more plumbers. He starts thinking (ambition) that he wants to branch out to

HVAC and Electrical work.

The plumber then attends some classes for basic understanding and certifications of electrical and HVAC. He then hires electricians and HVAC techs and expands his business into a one-stop shop for most construction companies. He is now 30 and owns a business that is worth well over a million dollars in annual income.

He did all of this on ambition and drive alone. I would be confident in saying that he has his fair share of 24-year-old Stacy Smokeshows lined up to pull him off the market. They know that if he is consistently growing then they will be very well taken care of if they can lock him down.

Regardless of what the media is telling you, most women do not want to be a "Boss Bitch" long term. Women are driven to have babies; it is in their genetics for the species to survive. Most women will go to college and make it about five years in a career before the fever hits. When that happens, their cave woman brain is driven to one thing, getting the best man to throw that baby batter in them. Some news for the few women that may be reading this book, men do not care about your career, it does not add to your value in his eyes.

The women's drive is so high for children, that some companies are offering benefits packages that include egg freezing and fertility treatments. This is an attempt to keep women in the workforce past the typical age of about 30 when most women are mothers and raising the children takes priority over their careers.

A direct correlation to her drive for children will be your drive to provide. If you marry a woman a few years younger that you, which is most cases, at 30 and her being 25. At 25, the fever is starting to rise and by the time she is 30, it is at dangerous levels, while you should be well established in your career and starting to see the fruits of your labor. At 35, you are probably a supervisor or manager and on the initial climb of your income potential. At this time, your providing capability will kick her baby fever into high gear.

The key to understanding is that ambition and drive will determine your ability to provide. You will need to make the right decisions with your ambition and follow up with the right actions.

She will watch what you do, so get your ass in gear. If you can't, then the women who want to marry, won't want to be married to you. Or you may be able to fake your way into a marriage with a good woman, but it won't last long, as you start to show that lazy, good-for-nothing behavior.

Another aspect to consider, you may have a million dollars in the bank, but could you take care of your family if society collapses? We don't mean that you go live in the wilderness and live off the land, but a little knowledge of how to hunt, get fresh water, and meet other basic needs could come in handy.

And if you are still holding on to your Safe World Theory, the least you could do is admit that history has shown that societies have collapsed in the past (Romans, Persians). If you want a chance to keep your family alive, you better know how to kill something (also see Protect).

Get a plan based on purpose early in life and work it to your grave.

Male RMV Preside

Here is the worst word (even with all the F-Bombs) in this material: Patriarchy. Your job as a man is to preside over the family unit, yes that means it is patriarchy. Yes, we know what everyone is saying, but the reality is that women don't want the responsibility or the accountability of a matriarchy. All they see are the perceived benefits and not the work.

As stated earlier, democracies need more than two people to exist. Relationships are unable to be democracies.

If an agreement cannot be reach about a topic, then everything grinds to a halt. Someone must take the responsibility and decide. That responsibility falls on you.

Accountability is kryptonite to women. Most women want to be given direction, it's just easier that way. You as the man in the relationship are the sole person responsible and you will be held accountable for the actions of all people in the relationship. If you don't believe it, talk to an involved father who has a child in the justice system at a young age. The parents pay more of a price than the child, and it's mostly the father who must bear the weight of the court's mandates.

For an example of lack of accountability, there are five parts to an effective apology for wrongdoing: expressing regret, accepting responsibility, making restitution, changing behavior, and requesting forgiveness. Admittedly, most people have problems with hitting all the requirements. However, in our experience, women are notorious for failed apologies.

Most women, just express regret with a simple "I'm sorry" and forget the issue ever happened. Some won't even go that far and not even acknowledge that the incident took place until you address it. Then it is immediately deflected by displacing blame. You may get a half-hearted apology, but you will find that the most important aspect, the change of behavior, is hard for a woman to accomplish.

For this reason, you must be the solely responsible figure in the family unit. You are the bringer of accountability. Uncle Ben in Spiderman got it partially right: "With great power comes great responsibility". There is also the flip side of the coin: "With great responsibility comes great power".

You must set and defend standards and boundaries for your family, you must be the asshole. No question, because if you don't then no one will. Being the asshole is not a 24/7 job, there are times when things can be smooth, but as soon as a boundary is crossed you must be there with swift attention.

If your son wants to go hang out with his friends and your boundaries are that his homework must be done, his room must be clean, and his chores completed. He will pull the classic, just ask mom, and she will say yes. You come home from work; he is gone without doing any of the requirements.

Swift attention is called for. Turn your ass around and bring your son back home. Say nothing to your wife, just walk away. Get in the car, find your son, and order him in the car. Drive back home without a word. When he is back home, instruct him to complete all the requirements, with few words as possible. That is all that needs to be done, maintain the standard. No need for yelling, ass chewing, or getting physical.

Your wife will correct herself; your son was just embarrassed if front of his friends and that will certainly make him think twice before pulling that shit again. Just that simple, it took five minutes to maintain the standard and you didn't have to act like you had an aneurism or a hissy fit.

Furthermore, it is imperative that the term "go ask your mom" never, under any circumstances comes out of your mouth. By doing so, you are giving your authority solely to her. If she decides to not maintain the standard or boundaries, then you must eat the outcome. Then you have a harder time in the future reestablishing the boundary in the future. You will also have to address the habits that this will form. Before you know it, you will have lost all control.

Your default answer to a request from anyone should be "No". The only caveat to this is needed (providing and protecting are needs of others). Needs are free, wants are earned. Defaulting to "no" will allow for time to ascertain if standards and boundaries have been met. Once the questions have been answered to standard, then you can change your answer to "yes".

As a rule, requests of children to parents should be made at least 24 hours in advance and the presence of both parents. More on parenting later. Understand that this allows you to maintain the standards until you can trust your wife not to shit on your work thus far. The pinnacle of a wife who is fully functioning as an FO is that you trust her to act as if you are standing next to her even when you are not.

Once you feel comfortable in not having to go snatch little Billy up from his friend's house to clean his room then the rule can be shit canned. But as soon as it happens again, you go right back to day one. You must tighten the chain slightly and leave it tight for a little while longer this time to ensure a good habit is formed.

All your actions will be an example to your son of what a husband and father should be. You will also be the bar for the future men in your daughter's life. If you're ok with your daughter marrying a complete tool, then go ahead and be a lazy ass in your household, fail to preside. Your offspring will emulate the behavior that you demonstrate.

Your ability to preside will be tested by women on the first date, if not before. If you think that a woman is going to go out with you if you can't plan a full date, then you are sadly mistaken. Well, she may go out, just for the free meal, but that's not why you are there. Your leadership in the early stages of the vetting process is directly correlated to your ability to preside over a family unit in a long-term relationship.

If you must ask Becky where she would like to eat on day one, you are starting behind the Eightball. She wants to see what decisions you are capable of. If you can't decide to take her to Red Lobster or Olive Garden, then how are you going to act when she wants a house that neither of can afford? Or getting your retirement accounts in order so that the two of you can live the rest of your days comfortably, instead of thinking that winning the lottery is your retirement plan.

A woman wants desperately to follow the lead of a strong man. You will be required to make the hard decisions and do the tough actions. Make no mistake, once established you cannot be wavering in your resolve to hold the line.

Once you decide, that is the decision until new information changes the view that you are not going to hit your intended outcome.

You don't have to bat a thousand and be right all the time. You need to decide with the information that you have available to you at the time. Then you must act based on the decision, then evaluate the outcome. If the outcome is less than desirable, change the decision. Men get wrapped into an endless loop of indecision. That will dry up even the wettest vagina.

You cannot be timid in your decision-making for fear of being wrong. Fuck, just be wrong, at least you did something. Once you realize you are wrong there is no harm in changing your decision for a better outcome. There is no need to apologize, just change the course, and get it done.

You will need people to follow you. They will not follow anyone that is scared to decide, they are also scared to decide. Just make one and go with it until it stops working, then make another decision. It is that simple, no need to over complicate a situation. Problems rarely ever solve themselves. You will need to take care of them.

For a happy and successful long-term relationship with healthy and productive offspring, you must do your absolute best to maximize your ability to protect, provide, and preside. Displaying them during the vetting process will ensure that you and your partner are a good fit.

FEMALE RELATIONSHIP MARKET VALUE

The female role in a relationship is to Manage, Multiply, and Motivate the other half to ensure the success of the long-term relationship. She must manage the day-to-day, take what is provided and multiply it, and motivate others to follow the strong lead of her partner.

Just like the Male RMV the Female RMV is no easy task. It can take decades to perfect. However, perfection is not the goal, improvement is. If his RMV is to protect, provide, and preside as the Captain, her managing, multiplying, and motivating is a complimentary part of the FO.

This is in line with the direction that he gives for the path of the family unit. The issue in the recent past and how this model has been discarded is in respect due to the Captain failing in his RMV. Even still how the Captain refused to stick to his guns and refuse to adjust to changing circumstances and/or environment.

The FOs rebelled and took over the ship. During the process, most Captains just quit and sat on the couch. The FO would nag, and the Captain would just do the bare minimum to return to the couch.

Your relationship success will be determined by how well

you maintain and improve your RMV and vet her against her RMV.

Female RMV Manage

Being the Captain is a full-time job. You can not be expected to handle all day-to-day activities and run your plan. The FO can assume this responsibility to free up your time to plan, decide, train, lead, and evaluate. Managing the daily chores is a key function of the FO. The estimated value of a stay-at-home spouse is $13 an hour. That comes out to $13,520 annually for a 40-hour work week.

However, the only time a stay-at-home spouse works 40 hours a week is when the family is on vacation. The estimated value that they contribute to the household could be better summed up as what you would pay for a service for the same results. If you hire a maid, chef, nanny, organizer, laundry service, etc. you would pay well over $40,000.

That is a large chunk of funds. If you are early in your plan and take home $80,000 annually, that is half of your salary. The question would then be what does your spouse bring home? Is it more that the low end of $13 or on the high of $40,000 annually?

It may be more beneficial for her to stay home and manage the day-to-day than to work. We caution if you are the husband, and you convince her to do so.

The family laws in your area may hurt you if the relationship goes south. You may be on the hook for alimony for the rest of your life.

However, if you are vetting properly, and improving

or maintaining your market value, then this should be unlikely. You must protect yourself in case you make a mistake. It is always a good idea to consult with a competent attorney before you even move in together. There are common law marriage laws in most areas and as soon as she uses the same address as you, you may be on the hook for more than you bargained for.

Once you find a high-value woman that you can rely on to bring along the journey with you (long-term), it would be a benefit for her to stay home and handle those daily activities. This will free up a lot this time and energy for both of you. I know that this sounds counter-intuitive, but if you are both working, who is cooking dinner, doing the laundry, or cleaning the house?

If it is both of you, your time and energy can be better spent at the iron church, leaning a new skill, running a side hustle, evaluating the current plan, and adjusting. Her time and energy could also be spent handling the daily requirements and could free her time when you are both available to join you in the more important activities that you are undertaking.

Vetting for this trait can be done simply by observing how she treats you in the early stages of the dating process. If she stays for a night of intense monkey sex, does she get up in the morning and make coffee and breakfast?

Or does she expect you to do it all like she is a princess that you should worship? How does she treat people that appear to have a lesser status than her, particularly those in the service industry?

If she talks down to waiters, cleaners, or any other people who provide a service that most of society looks down upon, she is not a high-value woman and is probably incapable of becoming one. She has probably learned this behavior from family members which means this is engrained in her. If you point the bad behavior out, she will just argue with you. This will waist more of your time on something that is not going to work out, just take the loss and move on.

Additionally, if she treats those in the service industry with disrespect, she will not be a productive stay-at-home spouse. She views those who perform a valuable service as lesser people, she will not "lower" herself to perform these things. She will probably pressure you to hire a maid or a nanny because of her views of this type of work. Not only will she be an additional mouth to feed but now you will be spending more money to maintain your standards. The only thing she brings at that point is a warm hole to shove your dick in. A prostitute would be a better return on investment.

<u>Female RMV Multiply</u>

"Whatever you give a woman, she will make greater. If you give her sperm, she'll give you a baby. If you give her a house, she'll give you a home. If you give her groceries, she'll give you a meal. If you smile at her, she'll give you her heart. She multiplies and enlarges what is given to her."

-      William Golding

This RMV trait is directly correlated to the man's ability to provide. If he is unable to give her a place to make a home, she is not living up to her full potential. If you give her shit ingredients, she can only polish a turd so much, you will get a shit meal. But, if you are living to your potential, she will feel compelled to live to hers. Only if you vetted properly in the dating phase.

From the beginning of time, the female of our species has always been able to create things for the family. She even can take what you make millions of a day (sperm) and combine it with what she makes once a month (her egg) and create offspring. Your sperm are expendable as you will continue to produce them well into old age. Her eggs on the other hand are not as plentiful. She will only produce about 300 in her lifetime. It is a stark comparison.

Creating offspring is the brainless function of this trait. It will happen naturally; all you need to do is drop enough baby batter in the womb. The other aspects are the ones that require some confirmation before you even think of giving her your DNA, if you make the wrong choice, you will have to deal with her for the rest of your life.

The specifics of how a woman will multiply what a man gives her are individual to the man. If a man does not need a clean home and prefers to do it himself. Then all he needs from her is to not create too much clutter so that he can do the cleaning. This is about the lowest of the bar. If a man prefers to cook, then she can gather the ingredients and he can do the chemistry part. Again, a low bar to hit. The vetting for this is not as stringent.

However, if a man would prefer a well-cooked meal most of the time and he is tired from running his plan, then it is more important for him to vet this trait out. If he prefers a clean house and would like to walk into one when he returns from a weeklong trip, then he needs to vet for this trait harder than the first man. You set the standard for your lifestyle, she can either live up to them or you don't need her.

Again, your return on investment would be better spent hiring a service than attempting to hold a woman that you are in a relationship with to your standards if she is unwilling or unable. This is a two-way street, you can gain her willingness and ability to multiply for you in simple yet increasing ways throughout the vetting process, however, you must maintain your end of the deal. Three P's and the three V's. Protect, Provide, Preside, SMV, RMV, and finally the JMV.

<u>Female RMV Motivate</u>

What is a high-value man? The making of a man, in general, has been measured for centuries by going to war, making a million dollars, or maybe working a dangerous job. The moment you become a man is the moment you become responsible for someone besides yourself. High-value men who practice emotional intelligence and self-discipline, can control their feelings and continuously focus on the purpose and plan.

Nick was a High valued man for 30-plus years. He was a United States Marine for 20-plus years and was in critical incident management for another 10 years. He was responsible for other Marines since he was 19 years old.

He is 50 years old now with three young kids, the oldest of which is 10. The 30-plus years of service no longer matter. Yes, allow your neighbor or your kids' teacher to thank you for your service, however, it means very little to the ones that receive the benefits. You can be everything to everyone, be a constant high-value man, and the second you stop, your value starts to reduce.

Meaning your effort and consistency in maintaining high value is eternal. Yes eternal, because the example you set for your kids to follow will continue to grow long after you are gone.

You need to be aware of the social conditioning that men have endured throughout time. It goes by many names but means the same thing; soul mates, the one, Mr./Ms. Right. The falsehood that one person is perfect for you, and you will cease to be able to exist if she leaves is programed into us by the media, the largest culprit in recent history is Disney and their damn princesses.

Not all women are the same, just as not all men are the same. However, you can find similarities in most people and most genders fall into generalized categories. You may be able to find rare personality traits, but you will have to dig very deep into someone's personality to find one that is not held by many others.

That point is being made so that you can understand that a woman's ability to motivate you and others through her overt and covert communication and behaviors is where she can stand out. Never enough that you will cease to breath if it ends. But this is where she can set herself apart form the crowd of mindless THOTs that you come across daily. This is where she really can shine and get that promotion.

You should be looking for her ability to motivate you to stay on target and work on the plan and motivate others to follow your leadership. It is that simple, but the impact is very high. If you promote the wrong woman, she can completely sabotage your plan. The power to sabotage is so extreme that you should think of Extinction Level

Event (ELO). She can take your whole existence. She can wield that much power.

Her motivation skills are again dependent on the self-discipline of the individual man. Some may need a woman to just stay out of the way, others may need a nudge a time or two. Her intuition should be able to make the nudges through covert communication. For example, if you are running the plan and raising the SMV, she will be saying yes more when you initiate intimate contact. On the flip side, she will deny more as you stray from progress, or you have given up all together thinking you crossed the finish line already.

Such is the importance of after-action reviews. You will need to know what she is trying to tell you through her actions. The only time she will openly communicate with you is when the "I love you, but I'm not in love with you" speech happens. Yes, it is a speech, not a talk. There is no debate or conversation, nothing you say is going to change the outcome of this speech. Just save some of your dignity and end it.

It is also important she motivates others to follow your lead. This is especially important with your children. This is most seen in the "Dad said no, so let's ask Mom" scenario. Hence both parents are present for the requests rule. She should be able to ask the same questions you would ask and give the same answer that you would give if you were not there. This shows a united front to the children and over time this kind of behavior will stop. The more she witnesses your actions in several scenarios with the children she will understand more of her role.

There is also the issue of what is spoken about you

behind your back. Women are notoriously catty; they talk about you amongst their peer group. Just know that there probably are no secrets. You will probably never know what is being said, she may tell you bits and pieces, but you will never get the whole truth. You can bet on that if you are not running your plan and striving to reach your max level of value. She is talking about it to someone!

If you think she is a nagging bitch, you have better believe that she is telling her friends that you are the bane of her existence. Probably in more colorful ways and language than you are reading here. If you are your highest value self, you better believe that she has nothing bad to say about you. She will even brag to her friends about you. They will reply how lucky she is to have you and how they wished their husbands could be half the man you are.

Vetting for this can be tricky, the easiest way is to just overhear conversations she has with peers. You can also be a good judge of how she interacts with her mother. If her mother is catty and talks shit about the neighbors, you can bet that this isn't the first time. Your potential mate has probably witnessed this most of her life. Her mother may have even talked shit about her father to her. Then there is no real hope for you. She will have a hard time motivating others for you as the opposite has been engrained in her since a young age.

Another way is to just listen to her vent. Women will need to vent about work, their friends, and just about anything. You can weight her reaction to the reasonableness of the issue. If she goes on an hour-long rant because her lunch order was on white instead of wheat, but only makes a passing comment about how great the ride in her new car is. She is negative-centric, and it will be challenging for her to properly motivate you or others in the way you may need.

The importance of vetting for her RMV before promoting too high up the ranks cannot be understated. She is doing the same to you, maybe unconsciously, but vetting your RMV all the same. There is no such thing as a perfect woman for a single man, so don't get hung up on her if she is throwing you red flags. Just let the plate fall off the stick, demote if necessary and move on. Your time is too valuable to just give it away for little in return.

In the previous chapters, we covered the SMV and RMV, as well as how to improve and vet for the best possible outcomes. In the next chapter, we will discuss the Relationship Mental Frame, or just Frame as it is commonly referred to. All your improvement and vetting mean nothing for a man if he cannot maintain the frame of the relationship.

FRAME – DOMINANCE AND SUBMISSIVE

Well, fuck. Now your triggered.

Words have meaning, that are determined by a collective not how they make you feel. To prove the point, the Oxford English Dictionary definitions are:

Dominance:

the fact of being more important, powerful or easy to notice than somebody/something else

political/economic dominance

dominance over somebody/something to achieve/assert/ establish dominance over somebody

Submissive:

willing to accept somebody else's authority and willing to obey them without questioning anything they want you to do

Now that the common terminology has been established, we can move past the fee fees and have rational thought. We hope that the definition proves that the words are not as bad as they made you feel. If you look at the application of the words in the form of a male/female relationship, which we are using here. A male is biologically more powerful than a female. Additionally, a female can decide to be unwilling to accept the male's biological power and size advantage. In this case she can leave. Adversely, the male can become tired of the female's unwillingness to accept the male's dominance and he can leave.

The Relationship Mental Frame can be best described as the person who controls the relationship. A relationship cannot be a 50/50 split. There is always a stronger leader in the relationship that has control due to the increased responsibility. The nagging wife to a lazy husband has the frame. The wife who controls her husband's free time, by telling him when he can spend time with his friends, has the frame. The wife who controls the family finances to the point the husband gets an angry phone call because she got an alert form the bank that he spent $10 on lunch, surely controls the frame. The husband who makes statements of "Let me ask my wife" and "My wife won't like it if I do that", has no frame.

We do not see that as a life lived by a high-value man. In those previous cases, these are probably men who have thought they reached the finish line and can coast until the grave. The wives have taken control of the relationship and are frustrated in the act of taking all the responsibility. These men can raise their value and return to the man that they used to be and regain the frame.

Most men at the beginning of the relationship demonstrated high value by displaying the SMV and RMV their wives loved, hence the marriage. Over time they just get comfortable as in their mind they made it, they have done everything that society has told them to. Get a job, get a house, get a wife, have some kids and you're done. This could not be further from the truth. Successful happy relationships work for both partners. One of them doesn't just get to quit or retire in place. The key is for the man to set the frame in the beginning (most do this naturally, especially if he is post-divorce) and maintain the damn thing until the grave.

Another way to understand the frame is the dominance and submission aspect of the relationship. We do not mean the kind with whips and leather, but the more natural state. Your life is full of dominance and submission relationships. For example, you accept government control, you accept your boss's control. Your kids, wife, and employees, all should be accepting your dominance.

Most frame relationships have a monetary exchange for the value of the submission. In personal relationships that exchange is provided through trust and performance (constant positive outcomes with increasing impact). The submissive person must trust that the dominant person is doing what needs to be done for the greater good and mutual benefit.

We propose a basic equation to understand how this type of relationship works in the psyche:

SMV/RMV +/- Performance +/- Trust = Submission

The equation for your professional career looks slightly different but similar:

Job Market Value (JMV) +/- Performance +/- Trust = Income.

We will explain both but start with the career equation first. Your JMV is equivalent to your SMV/RMV, it just applies to the workplace. JMV is a collection of your education, experience, and leadership. Your performance can be explained as your outcomes and impact. Just as in personal relationships, there are negative and positive outcomes, and these have increasing degrees of impact on the work environment.

If you work for a small company with a net worth of five million and bring in a client on a 10-year contract with an annual sales total of one million. You just added a 20% increase to the overall net value for the next 10 years. That is a positive outcome with a huge impact. This action just gained you the trust of the boss, who now has a safety net to take bigger risks. You are now the golden child of this small business. That will relate to a higher status position in the company with a raise.

The same would apply to the negative. If you lost that client after the first year of the contract, through negligence or incompetence resulting in a breach of contract, this is a negative outcome with a high impact. Your boss has less trust in you and now you must go through the arduous task of rebuilding it. If you can't build it fast or high enough, or if the impact is too high, your boss may break up with you (fire you).

This same mindset applies to personal relationships, for what is a divorce or breaks up but one person firing another?

You must build that trust throughout the vetting (dating) process by demonstrating your SMV/RMV and getting more positive outcomes with increasing impact. That is how you both decide to promote each other. Where most relationships fail in the marriage stage is that one or both think they have reached the finish line and do the bare minimum to keep their job. This reduces positive outcomes, understand that the reduction in positive outcomes drags the impact to a halt, much like turtles stampeding through peanut butter.

You must stay on target, work on the plan, and increase impact through positive outcomes. Just as in your career, if you get a promotion, you must work to increase your boss' trust in you. You will need to do that for your wife, or she will fire you and take half your shit as a severance package with the possibility of royalties for life (alimony).

A wife that sees steady positive outcomes with good impacts will trust that you are right. You have demonstrated that you are a man of action, she will blindly follow you into the deepest pits of hell. This is required for her submission to your dominance. For you to maintain frame her submission is vital.

Words mean nothing to her if the source is someone lacking in emotional intelligence and self-discipline. You can tell her this is where the plan will take the two of you and she will not believe a word of it if you have failed to demonstrate you are worthy of her submission. She will constantly buck your frame until you prove that you can do it on your own. Honesty, could you blame her? You must have done enough to gain her acceptance in the dating phase, but you probably did it unconsciously, and you didn't after-action the process. Then do it now. It is a simple as asking yourself "Am I the man that she first met and then married? Am I better or worse?". That should be enough to get you started.

You can then begin the process to review the environment or status and how it has changed. As time progresses, if you are running the plan then your impact should be increasing, then you can take less of a micro-management approach to the household. The higher the impact the more time and energy are needed to maintain and increase. If you are stuck in having to lead the family in day-to-day functions, you can't get to your plan. You will be trapped in an endless cycle of starting, stopping to put out a fire, attempting to reestablish the frame, an argument ensues, and your day is over. You will never make any progress; we will cover how to deal with similar situations later.

Your relationship is dependent on you controlling the frame. You probably started that way; you just didn't know what you were doing. Women desire dominance and need the male frame to prosper. It is simply setting and maintaining standards and boundaries. Surely, in the beginning, your then-girlfriend did something that violated the standards and/or boundaries. Then you pointed it out and she corrected it. That was you holding frame or dominance. That is what she wanted.

Over time your laziness, incompetence, or your social programing settled in, and you stopped addressing minor violations. Then later the minor violations turned into larger violations, and now you may be facing major violations. You have lost frame by a thousand cuts. You may have even tried to push back which started an argument. That argument may have lasted days until you finally caved and just gave in.

Your relationship may now be in a state where you don't matter past your paycheck. Now that if you get laid off, you no longer bring anything to the table and the only reason she hasn't left you yet is that there is not a better option, YET. That better option could come around tomorrow, and there goes half your shit. All because you took the easy route and didn't maintain the frame.

SMV and RMV will get you a marriage to a high-value woman, but your ability to maintain frame, will be what keeps it together. That will require her submission, which is dependent on the relationship equation.

If you do not have a set of standards yet, get some. You can do this by imagining what the perfect environment would look like for the highest impact of your plan. Do you need a clean house to function? That's a standard. Do you need meals prepared while you increase your gravitational pull? That is a standard. Do you need a space of your own to pray and work on your side hustle? That is a standard, create the space then put a sign on the door. But that's not enough, there are speed limit signs and people still speed. You need to police (enforce) your signs, just another way of saying maintain your frame.

Once you have your standards, you need to set your boundaries. These are hard and fast rules that you, her, and any future offspring will need to live by. They are larger in importance, if you use standards as a speed limit sign, then boundaries are reinforced concrete walls. There may be wiggle room in standards dependent on the environment, there is no room for fuck ups in boundaries.

Your boundaries should follow your values. For example, if you are fully following your genetic drive to impregnate even women of age in the world, then a boundary of monogamy is going to directly conflict with your view. If you set that boundary to satisfy a woman who demands it, you are either not living to your purpose, which will suck for all of eternity, or you are going to disregard and cheat. There goes half your shit. A better boundary would be a commitment to non-monogamy. Then you will need to vet for that in the women you date.

Another example is that if you set a boundary to never mix your finances (which we highly recommend), then if you cave and give her a credit or debit card on your account, you have just submitted to her frame. If your boundaries can be nagged enough for you to cave, then your standards don't mean much.

If she needs money, which she will if she is a stay-at-home spouse supporting your work on the plan. You can transfer money to her account or have a shared account that you can transfer money into. To maintain your boundary, ensure that your income is deposited to your primary account and not the shared account. This is still maintaining the frame and coming to a compromise.

The most consistent way to establish and maintain a frame is to call bullshit. Standards and boundaries are tested in mainly two ways:

1. Unreasonable Requests
2. Unreasonable Tone

You will need to address these immediately, as your frame is being tested at face value. We will go further in-depth in a later chapter. But unreasonableness should be a boundary. When either of these issues arises, it is all-stop.

An unreasonable request could be several things, but

they can be classified as anything that is pulling you off your plan that can not be easily completed. I.e., you are requested to drive across town to drop off her lunch that she forgot for work on your day off. This will take over two hours of your day while you have a meeting with your mentor scheduled. You will have to reschedule your meeting and drop off her lunch, you are now paying for her consequences. That is unreasonable.

You are getting ready to head to the iron church, which you do every day at 2 PM, she stops you and wants to tell you about what Kathy from marketing did to her today. Your standard is that you leave for afternoon services at church at 2, EVERY SINGLE DAY. She wants you to delay, which can easily turn into not going. That is unreasonable.

Or she requests for you to stop mowing the lawn to help her hang a shelf. To be clear this will only take five minutes, not pulling you from your plan for an extended period. However, she uses an unreasonable tone. For example, "Come help me hang this shelf". Unreasonable.

If you two are having a conversation, and she gives you "Can you get to the point". This is not only unreasonable but also overt communication. Women do not overtly communicate, only when it is necessary, they much rather communicate covertly. This is a much larger issue than the tone, you will need to call bullshit on the tone, but also Own Your Shit. There is something that you did that she thinks it is fine to speak to you in that manner as if her time is more important than yours. You are probably not running your plan and/or not producing enough positive outcomes and impact.

PURPOSE AND PLAN

"Don't be silly, there is no boy here."

- Arthur Rackham, Jack and the Beanstalk, 1734

Purpose, calling, direction, objective, and mission can be interchangeable as a description of what gets you out of bed in the morning for the rest of your life. Your purpose needs to be bigger than your career, bigger than your family, bigger than your current self. If it is not, you will be one of those men who dies six months after retirement or within months of his wife dying. If your purpose is contingent on others or specific things, once it is gone, it won't be there to get you out of bed.

It should be short and sweet. One or two words. If it is a sentence or paragraph, that is a vision statement, not a purpose. It should also represent your drive and ambition, not just in your career but in your life. If you set your purpose to "Greatest Father", what will you do when your kids are grown? Your purpose needs to be something that you will consistently strive to achieve for your entire adult life.

Your purpose is the starting point, your plan is your path. For example, you have decided your purpose is to "Serve Through Growth". This can be achieved through multiple paths, some being simultaneous and parallel. You can serve through the military or another civil service. You can also serve by mentoring others. This is hitting both aspects of your purpose.

Later in life, you retire from the military, and your purpose doesn't change, just your plan. You can then serve in the fire service or law enforcement. Or just start your own consulting business and coach others. Your purpose is still the same, the only thing that changed is how you do it. You may then decide that you can best serve by entering the political arena. Again, the purpose remains constant, and plans change.

Once you establish and define your purpose, then you set your path from your current spot to a destination in the far future, roughly 10 to 20 years. This should be in direct support of your purpose. You will need to evaluate and adjust to changing conditions as needed. This is a good starting point to set goals.

Goals should be set that directly support your plan. These are projects that should be broken down into 1-, 3-, and 5-year increments. The short term (1 year) should be most of your goals, the mid-term (3 years) should be fewer, and the long term (5 years) should be the least. The short term should support the mid, which should support the long-term goals. You don't want a dozen long-term goals, every five years you will be scrabbling to hit the mark. Not a very good way to accomplish things.

All other things that require less than a year to complete can be broken down into tasks or just to-dos. Tasks are more labor intensive and can take up to months to complete. To-dos are not as labor intensive and are completed in a short term. These are the day-to-day activities. To-dos are best to have delegated in the early stages of a relationship. Tasks can start being delegated later when standards are maintained when she completes to-dos.

Once you get all this set and you have committed to it. You must make the purpose and plan your TOP priority. Anything that doesn't directly support your plan or path needs to be delegated to free up time and energy for activities that produce positive outcomes. As time and your ability progress, higher impact activities are going to consume more time and energy. So, as you progress, your support needs to progress as well. The delegated to-dos and tasks are going to become more challenging as your goals become more challenging for you.

Therefore, maintaining SMV/RMV, Performance, and Frame is so important. As you grow on your path, she will need to grow and become more proficient as well. You are never going to hit your goals if you are too consumed with maintaining your frame. If you need her to do a task and it turns into an argument, you are now pulled off your path to deal with the argument and then complete the task yourself.

What a waist of your valuable time and energy. Energy is like money, you can always make more, time however is finite, and you will never get any back. You can learn how to be more proficient in how you use your money and energy. You can only learn how to manage your time. If you are wasting your time arguing about shit that does not matter, then you will never get anything done. The next chapter will give guidance on how to deal with these types of scenarios.

Women do not want to be the center of your universe.

They want you to be a man on a mission, doing important shit and making an impact in the universe. The only way to do this is to prioritize your plan and work the fucking hell out of it.

Jack and the Beanstalk

The fairy tale of Jack and the Beanstalk, like most fairy tells, is a metaphor for life. If you can do more than just listen or read the damn thing it has many life lessons for boys and men. It is ultimately a story of a boy becoming a man. Jack is given a task; he makes a stupid childish decision to trade the cow for "magic beans" in place of food. He is scolded and goes to bed hungry, forced to face his consequences. But his mother must face his consequences as well, as she doesn't get to eat either. His mother in her anger throws the "magic beans" out the window.

Jack wakes up to a massive stalk and decides to climb. The stalk represents a boy's journey to higher knowledge and experience. When he gets to the top, a bunch of shit happens that does not concern us currently. He steals some important stuff and climbs down with the giant in pursuit.

When Jack reaches the bottom. He makes his first manly decision and recognizes that if the giant can reach the bottom, havoc will ensue, and he will be responsible. He "Owns His Shit", picks up an axe, and chops the stalk down killing the giant. The act of chopping down the stalk is a metaphor for a man owning his shit, planning with his purpose in mind, and acting. Resulting in a positive outcome, with an extremely high impact as if the giant made it down there would be much property damage and loss of life. What does Jack get out of all of this besides another day above ground?

You forgot about what Jack stole. A Goose that lays golden eggs, A Harp that plays on its own, and in many versions, a Princess. Not only are the items metaphors, but the order in which he obtains them is important as well. The Goose represents a career, the Harp represents a calling (or purpose), and the Princess represents a life partner.

Jack steels the Harp first, which starts yelling for the giant. Jack soothes the Harp, which now belongs to him. Jack bolts for the door, and as he flees, he swipes the Goose. Then runs across a cell with the Princess inside, gets the key (the key to her heart?) and flings open the cell door. Now Jack has a calling and a shit ton of money. You guessed it, Princess's panties vanish into thin air, and she gives chase to him, and the giant just must only follow her dripping body fluids.

The order is key in that most men find a calling and start making money as they gain mastery of the calling, then the woman comes into play as Jack will need help with his calling. In the story, the Princess is submissive and forever grateful to Jack for saving her from the giant and a life trapped with him. It didn't hurt that Jack had endless gold. You can assume that Jack will maintain and improve his SMV/RMV, Performance, and Frame because they live happily ever after. Which is, as you have learned by now, the only way to live happily ever after.

If Jack didn't at least maintain those things, the Princess would have taken the house. Jack would have been ordered to pay half of the golden eggs to her for the rest of his life by the King. He would have to set up in a one-bedroom apartment until he got past his anger. He would then be pressured to get back out on the market by his mother, because "every man needs a woman". All he could find would be single moms whose kids "are her world" and live out the rest of his life in monotony.

The order in which Jack steels the items is not only representative of the men's growth timeline. It is more importantly a representation of the order of importance. Jack's calling comes first, through his mastery (soothing and playing the Harp), he gets paid for his value (the Goose). Only then does the Princess enter the picture. Those should be the order of a man's priorities.

Your calling comes first. You must plan to master your purpose, then you will start receiving money for your mastery, which is a representation of your value. Then, and only then will you be able to get the submission of a high-value woman.

If you are maintaining your SMV/RMV, Performance, and Frame, she will support your endeavors and you can delegate your tasks and to-dos to her. She will happily complete them often to higher standards than yours.

She will do this because you are the prize. You are the reward for her labors. Your time and attention are her currency for her value. This is key. You master your calling and get paid for it, she masters supporting your plans, and you reward her with your priceless time and attention.

If you are solely focused on your plans, any time you give to her is a reward. Do not just give it away for free. It must be earned. Therefore, it is important not to reward her bad behavior. If she is meeting your wants and needs, according to your plans, then reward her. If she is not, don't give her your time or attention by arguing about it. This is where most men fail and allow her to pull him off his path. This most often happens in the stages when a lazy husband starts to reestablish the frame by enforcing standards and boundaries.

John had a "relationship" that lasted over a year. During that time, she begged and pleaded for a promotion, but never left him. The promotion never came, his response was always, "That's not going to happen, consider this you're training to be a fantastic wife one day, but not to me. The next serious relationship you have, if you keep treating him the way you treat me, he will marry you".

A few years after he called it off, she reached out to him to let him know that she was now married with a child, just as he said it would be. That was the overt communication, the covert communication was as you guessed it. She was not getting what she wanted from her now husband, she missed the masculine frame that trained her and the unflinching devotion to his purpose that made her panties fall off.

Women desire a man following his purpose. She will move mountains for him, she will sacrifice everything to ensure that he succeeds. His success is HER success. She will do anything and everything he requests. If you retain nothing from the pages here, remember this and follow it till your dying breath. You may not get the Princess that Jack got, but you will make the world in your image. And that goose will shit out plenty of gold for you.

SHIT TESTS VS COMFORT TESTS

In the last chapter, we glossed over unreasonable requests and unreasonable tone. These actions can be called a Shit Test. They may be conscious or unconscious as women will periodically test you to ensure you are still maintaining your frame. A Shit Test is ultimately a test of your SMV.

This is where most men lose the battle throughout the relationship. Over time they react to a shit test as if it were a Comfort Test (more on this later). A Shit Test is a test of your, as some would call it "Alpha" traits. A Comfort Test is a test of your "Beta" traits or testing of your RMV.

Shit and Comfort Tests have very different responses. The key is to understand what is being presented, then react properly.

Shit Tests

There are two ways to identify a Shit Test:

1. A Standard is not met, or a Boundary is crossed
2. The unreasonableness of Request or Tone

That's it, simple. The phycology is not. Once a woman

has bought into your SMV/RMV and has agreed to support your plans through support to your standards. She will also agree to your boundaries and enforce them to others for you. Understand that she is all in, you are her future, and it is a great responsibility. This is the female form of Oneitis.

Her hypergamous nature is going to need reassurance that you are still the best option for her. Therefore, from time to time you will get Shit Tested in one of the two ways previously mentioned. You need to acknowledge the behavior and stop any further conversation. This is best done in one sentence. For example, you have a standard that you need to have a healthy dinner and since she didn't work that day, you asked for a special meal that she has prepared in the past. You also requested it at a certain time as it would give you enough time to eat with her and get back to some pressing business.

She fails to deliver as requested and its time for dinner and there is no movement in the kitchen. You can make a simple statement such as "Where's dinner?". This will cause her to get defensive and she will overreact. Her mental hamster will start spinning and she will come up with excuses, place blame, or deflect by turning it around on you. Then you will react to her behavior with something like "What are you taking about?".

Then you can practically see the steam start to billow from her ears. Now the fight is on, you screwed the pouch on this one. Before you know it, an hour has gone by, you're both pissed off as hell, and neither of you has eaten. To add insult to injury, now you're so angry, you can't focus on what needs to be done and you lose productivity for the rest of the night.

The better option is to just clearly identify the behavior in one sentence, like "I needed that dinner at that time, I am going back to work, come get me when it's ready". The impactful action is walking away! The conversation is over, maintain radio silence. Go back to your new, more productive "Man Cave" and go back to work. Do not respond to anything else besides "Dinner is ready".

Allow the process to happen. Allow her to try and engage as you walk away, just ignore it. It doesn't matter, what you need is her to support you as you asked. She will eventually stop and come to her senses. She will know that she created a problem for you, and she knows how to fix it. How she fixes it doesn't matter to you, the only thing that matters is that it is fixed. On the other side of this coin is the alternative lack of action and that doesn't require a response from you or an explanation from her.

By doing the above, you have enforced the standard and removed any more time or attention to it. This enforces your commitment to your purpose while enforcing standards. It is now up to her to live up to the standard that was set. If she doesn't then when you are done working. Get your shit and go out to eat alone. With out saying a word, you are not trying to hurt feelings or poke the bear.

This action gets everyone what they want. You wanted a healthy dinner so that you could continue to get things done.

You did just that, it would have been nice for her to help, but not a requirement. She didn't want to take the time, expend the energy, or thought something else was more important. She also got what she wanted, she didn't have to, and she got to keep doing the more important thing. All of this without an argument.

Now, understand for the first few times you do this, she will try to start the argument or a similar one soon. That's fine. You won't participate. If she starts getting pissy and you start seeing a warning sign. Cut it off with "I have to get something done". Again, walk away and get something done. Radio Silence and ignore all incoming transmissions.

You can not correct her behavior, you have no control over anyone else's, just your own. You are not giving time and attention to bad behavior. You only reward good behavior with time and attention. If she wants the time and attention, then she will correct the bad behavior.

We know, "this sounds very manipulative". You get what you put in. You gain the actions that your current value is worth. If you sit on the couch all day, not living your purpose, does she engage you often with sexual contact? Didn't think so. She is ignoring bad behavior.

Don't get mad about it, don't let it hurt your feelings (No one cares, and no one is coming to help). Just know it exists and use the tool as it is intended to be used.

There are scientific studies on positive reinforcement in dog training. How do you think the whales at Sea World are trained? Positive reinforcement.

Another way to handle a Shit Test is the Agree and Exaggerate technique. This is done when you hear a smart-ass comment, usually as, "You think she's hot don't you" or the classic "Stop staring at her tits/ass". The best way to respond is the Agree and Exaggerate, for the first example of that woman's hotness, "Sure do, I want to make her walk funny for days". That's it, no more conversation about it. For the second one, "I would love to, but all I want to do is motorboat them/it". Done, crisis everted. She will take it as a joke and laugh it off, and you didn't reward bad behavior.

So, stop rewarding bad behavior with negative reinforcement. Meaning stop arguing with her. Don't engage, don't reward her effort, and afford her to bring up the past! There is no benefit to either of you. Show some damn leadership and restraint and just not participate. You don't win anything. Not even the fight, she will not give you a trophy, you have just won the battle but lost the war. She will not suddenly understand your rational argument and stop you with a sexual reward. You will not get a cookie, a back rub, a homecooked meal, or a foot massage if you win an argument with her. Rest assured she will not let you sleep with her hot younger sister. You get nothing by participating.

Just maintain standards, ignore the reaction until the standard is met by doing something else, then reward the standards being met with your time and attention. That is the only positive way to respond to Shit Tests. Anything else is a failure. Sprinkle some Alpha on that steak and move on, let her eat it.

If you are a man in a long-term relationship that has slowly given up the frame and wishes to get it back the best thing you can do initially is just Shut the Fuck Up (STFU). Stop being a girlfriend to her, stop being all catty with her over a glass of wine. If you must sip on some whiskey while she tells you about her day. Give a few "yep" and "uh-huh", even throw in a clarifying question or two to make it seem like you're listening. Don't talk shit about her boss or Karen from sales, let her do all of that. Just STFU and listen.

No, she doesn't want you to fix it for her, she just wants you to listen. Just do that (meaning STFU). Let her get it off her chest, while you are thinking of what you are going to do when she is done. When she stops seeing you as a girlfriend, then she can start treating you like a man.

Then you can start to STFU. Give direction in as few words as possible and move on to something else. That's it, say your piece, STFU, and go about your plan. And remember, stop talking about your fee fees, no one cares. If she doesn't get the guidance or request done to the clearly defined standard. Let her know you don't like it and walk away. Done. Shit test passed.

A vital key to understanding this process is to know that male and female problems are intrinsically not the same. Women will not be able to understand the male problems. They do not understand the constant heartache of letting people down or the constant ache of failing another person who counted on you. The cost of one man failing another has higher costs than a woman can understand. This is biological, as historically, men have been more dependent on other men in high stake environments. A man's best friend is the man in the fox hole with him.

Do not try to regain the frame in a single conversation, and for fucks sake do not tell her what you are doing, just do it. You don't need to give her a power point on your actions to get the frame back and how she will appreciate it. She doesn't care. Just STFU and run the plan. Maintain standards and boundaries, she will understand, and she will be happier for it.

Comfort Tests

Comfort Tests are the testing of your RMV. These are sometimes brought on by too much dread. Remember that too much dread will have her question if you are committed to her and not straying. If you are in a committed monogamous relationship, she will be reassured that you are not going to trade her in for a newer model.

Comfort Tests also arise when she is feeling insecure about her status with you. Again, she is recognizing that you are a man of purpose, and she feels that you are deserving of a better woman. This will come across as a "Are you happy?" type of question.

You can easily respond to the first kind (dread induced) by simply ensuring that you are providing the benefits of lower relationship ranks. Question yourself, when was the last time you treated her like a girlfriend and ordered what she wears and when to wear it? Then reward her behavior with a night out followed by amazing sex. If it's been a couple of weeks, then get it done, you are starting to neglect her.

Therefore, you don't ask her if she is happy, you are displaying your dread. She will take the question as you need her. This will be conducive to you running your plan and living to your purpose. It also displays to her that she is your focus which is a low-value display. Display high value and stop displaying low value. Display high value by increasing your SMV/RMV, Performance, and Frame.

If you are still regularly providing the lower relationship

rank benefits and you are getting these types of Comfort Tests as in reasonable requests in reasonable tones. To correctly pass these tests all you must do is comply. That's it, just do it. She will feel that you are still committed to her, and the dread will dissipate. Just throw some beta at her, she will appreciate it and her hamster will go back to sleep, leaving her with the warm fuzzies.

The insecure type of Comfort Test, it is slightly more complicated. You are so high value that she feels that she does not deserve you. This requires encouragement. If she is going to church with you, let her know that you are seeing results and you couldn't be happier. Let her know how happy you are with the state of the house. Congratulate her on an utterly fantastic meal. Bonus points for the "mmmmmmm, so good" as you chew the first bite. And extra credit for some caveman grunts as you go in for a second bite of that steak or chicken.

Of the two, Comfort Tests are easier to handle as you have been conditioned to react this way most of your life. The Shit Tests are where you need to put some thought and consideration into a proper response. These are going to be more challenging because you have not practiced this behavior long-term. You may have unwittingly been this suave in the beginning but fell back into your conditioned ways with just a little bit of comfort.

Purpose and Plan take priority, do not waste time and attention on her dribbling incoherence. Just maintain standards and boundaries, this should pass the Shit Tests.

In the next chapter, we will cover the evaluation process known as After-Action Reviews. These are key to gaining valuable data to ensure that your plan will get the highest valued results.

FIELD TESTING AND AFTER-ACTION REVIEWS

In military organizations around the world, the process to create and maintain solders is one of:

1. Training to standard
2. Field Testing
3. After-Action Review
4. Retraining or advanced training
5. Repeat steps 2 through 4 until dead or retired

This process has worked for millennia by better men than you, no need to reinvent the wheel, use it for yourself.

Step 1 Training

This step is covered throughout this book. You need to apply this step to raising your SMV/RMV, Performance, and Frame. Pray at the Iron Church, expand your knowledge and experience, make more money, create a new business, pass some Shit Tests, and reestablish previous rank benefits are all examples of training.

Step 2 Field Testing

Now you have made gains at the altar of Mars, lost

some weight, adding some distance in the golden ratio. Now what, run some game on some women in the wild. Initiate, Isolate, and Escalate. Remember the warning for married men, no movement past Initiate if you like half your shit.

Now, record the reaction you get and the specifics from whom. Did she want to jump your bones right there and then or was it more of a polite exchange? Did she initiate physical touch? Or give off defensive body language. Did you get a win with physical touch and a little innuendo?

All this needs to be evaluated. In an honest and objectionable way as possible for you. A Board of Directors (covered in the next chapter) can offer a plethora of assistance in this area. Once you record all the data. Yes all, the good and the bad, even the seemingly insignificant.

You need to compile notes known as Field Reports. They are clear concise notes that contain all the information needed to move to the next process. They only contain facts. They do not contain assumptions or inferences either. The 4Ws+H (Who, What, When, Where, and How) The Why is going to be determined in the next step in the process.

Step 3 After-Action Review (AAR)
The AAR is a no-bullshit assessment of where you are today, what have you done to improve, and how did you test your training. Then you need to have a come to Jesus with yourself (AKA Owning Your Shit). Look at all the factors and what could be improved to get a better result.

Where you dressed like a slob when you attempted to run some game? Rookie mistake. Did you violate the golden rule of the Iron Church and hit on a female parishioner? Blasphemy, 10 Hail Mary's, and 20 Our Fathers. Did you run a field test on a girl with higher SMV than you and get shut out?

You need to keep your feelings in check (no one cares, no one is coming) and be brutally honest with your failures. You also need to approach your wins with humility. You are not in the grave yet, you can always to better. If you did a shit job of vetting, you may need to do better soon.

This assessment will give you your rough areas so you can smooth them and rough up some of those smooth areas. Your Board of Directors can help with covering your blind spots and give you a different perspective. It is vital not to brush off any result or reason. You must have good data and process with honest intent.

You can not sugar coat this process. If you are a fucking turd, be a fucking turd, just be one who is getting his shit together. If you are a rock star, be a rock star, but understand that you are not at the level of Mic Jagger, get better. If you are in uniform, it maybe you just ran a game on a Badge Bunny, Barracks Princess, or a Hose Humper. Any of them would gladly ride anyone in the same uniform. Be honest with yourself.

Compile a result of:

1. What went right
2. What needs improvement (most to least improvement)
3. What needs to be maintained

Step 4 Retraining or Advanced Training
Once you have your true results from your AAR.

Give yourself a P.O.B. (Pat on the Back) for what was right. Make or adjust your plan to tackle the needs improvement areas, starting with the needs most improvement. Plan to maintain what you have in the right maintenance areas.

Get to work. Don't make excuses, lay blame, or ignore the results because they hurt your fee fees. That's what women and children do. You are a man on a mission, run the mission and stay on target.

Set a reasonable deadline for improvement (retraining), with an actual calendar date as a goal. I will drop five more pounds in two weeks. Then get to work. Once you meet the goal at the deadline. Move to the next step.

Step 5 Rinse and Repeat

Now that you have hit your goal produced by your AAR including retraining, you need to start at Step 2 and Field Test again. Then run through the AAR and retrain. You will need to do this until you take your last breath. You will not see the finish line.

This process should be run on any activity you do that effect your SMV/RMV, Performance, or Frame. The wife shit tests you; you respond, how do you know if it worked or not? AAR. You hit on the hot Becky from accounting, you have wild monkey sex in the copy room. AAR. You complete a part of your plan at the 1-year goal. AAR that shit.

There is no point in doing anything if you don't learn from it. This function is just as important as all the others. You should be performing this function in all aspects of your life. If you are dropping weight and focusing on strength increases at the Church. How are you recording your progress? How do you know if you are making gains if you are not recording and then comparing results? The weight coming off is not a representation of strength.

If you are running a project to increase your income by 20% in the next five years. How are you recording your progress? Are you just looking at your bank account? How do you know if your actions over the last six months have moved you closer to the goal? How far did you move to that goal? In six months are you already at 15%, do you need to raise the goal? Is the current growth pattern sustainable?

All these questions can be answered if you are running a Field Test and AAR system. You will have no idea if what you are doing is a waste of time. And always remember that your time and attention are what value you give to important things in your life. If you are not giving your time and attention to the entire process, you could be screwing your self and not even knowing it.

You may already be doing a version of this in a more casual format. You may talk about it with your buddies (Your Board of Directors), and you may get some feedback. But how do you know if the feedback is good? Are you giving them all the information or just what you deem to be important?

You need to structure the process, get organized and start swapping notes with the Board. This will get you your best data. Shit in = Shit out. If you can't work the process to completion, you will get bad data and make bad decisions. This is wasting every minute that you spent on the program or energy spent attempting to gain success on a goal.

If you work the AAR process in its entirety you will get good data and make better decisions. This will be the first step in managing your time better. You will notice a lot of free time opening for you to tackle bigger projects with better outcomes and higher impacts. If you are praying at church in a manner that is not giving you results and you are spending two hours at the gym. The process will show you that. You can adjust to a program that only takes an hour. Run the process again, and you find you get better results in half the time.

Now you have a full hour to focus on something else. That hour could be used to give back some of the lower-ranked benefits to your wife. Like a nice night out followed by wild sleazy motel room sex that knocks pictures off the walls. A win-win. All because you spent some time making good conscious decisions.

THE BOARD OF DIRECTORS

Your friends that you discuss your problems in life are, what we consider, your Board of Directors. These are men with like minds. They can part wisdom from their own experiences. We live in a world full of knowledge, experience, and wisdom. What's better is that never in history have you had this much access to that wisdom. You can find an answer to almost any question at the touch of a button.

Admittedly, most of the answers you find on the internet are just shit diatribes. But you can filter out the nonsense and apply what works. Your Board on the other hand are trusted advisers. You have vetted them and run some AARs by them with good results in the past. You have no reason to believe that they would steer you wrong in the future.

There was a time when these Boards would meet in a more formal setting in designated places reserved for such activities. These were known as Men's Clubs. No, not the one with mostly naked nursing students, "working" their way through college.

The real ones, with leather chairs, whiskey glasses, cigars, and a dress code. Sadly, with the new wave of feminism, these very valuable places are not allowed by society or have been invaded by women.

"But what's the problem with that?" you ask. Simple, once a woman is allowed into the male space. The Male mind in that space changes from a helpful mindset to a sexual mindset. This produces male completion.

This is completely unconscious, the overall intent for that group is dead, you're just waiting on the competition for her attention to start.

The unconscious male competition will pit one against the other, and they will start slowly offering less helpful advice. Soon, there will be others who start siding with the female to gain favor with her. Then sides will be chosen. The Alphas will double down on the male competition, the Betas will double down on the gaining favor behavior.

The group is then pitted against one another like an episode of Survivor. It is no longer about helping men, but about getting attention from her. And, no, it doesn't matter what she looks like if this happens or not. Her appearance only dictates the timeline of the eventual fall of the group. It will happen no matter what. It is our biology; you can't fight it.

A male group that allows just a few women in is the replica of our early social groups. Many men with very few fertile females. It is wise to follow the rules that our father's set before us if we don't understand the reason for the rule in the first place.

There is a story behind every rule. The reason for the "No Swimming" sign on the bank of a pond with a gator lying under it, is because someone was eaten. The reason for the "No Women Allowed" sign on the door of a Men's Club is because men's biology from a bygone age is to prevent nursing students from going in there and fucking things up for the rest of us. The reason the same sign needs to be on your workspace is to prevent distractions. The "No Women Allowed" sign is enforced to prevent distractions from the work that men and only men must accomplish. Recall that women don't understand the male problems of the world.

These Clubs of old had strict membership rules and extensive vetting processes. The reason for that is to not waste the time of more successful men who had been there and done that and were willing to pass on their knowledge. If you were a bus boy, you were not going to get directions from a Rockefeller. You had not earned that privilege yet. You must earn access to great minds.

The same bus boy could get guidance from a group of Restaurant Managers, as they would be willing to give him some time. But a high-value man would not waste his valuable time on someone who would not listen and rise to the same level. Yes, this sounds quite antiquated and bigoted. But it is truthful and necessary.

You see, you are the sum of your Board. If five of your friends are addicts, you will become the sixth. You may be able to rise slightly above the other five but your mere association with them will pull you down. You will not be able to rise much higher until you cut the line of those anchors. Why would a high-value man want to associate with someone who will pull him down?

Your Board must be vetted to the same high standards. If you surround yourself with lesser men, you are gaining nothing from the relationship. If they were plates you were spinning that you gain nothing from, you would drop the plates like a bad habit. You should never be the smartest or most successful man in the room for very long. If you are, you are in the wrong room.

You should also be careful as to who you take advice from, if you would not switch roles with a man, then his advice should be considered suspect. You should fill spots on your board with at least half men with which you would happily switch places. Men who constantly complain about their lives, wives, and children are going to corrupt your mindset over time.

They will offer you shit advice so that you will mirror their actions. If you do not admire them whatsoever, then no need to heed their advice. If you are not getting wisdom and guidance from your Board, then you need to clean the house. Demote them like you would a bad woman and fill the void they leave with better options. You are no longer in school; you get to pick your teachers and not just be stuck with the ones the school board gave you.

You need the main man on that board, a majority shareholder. This man is your mentor. He is the one who gives the best sage advice on most aspects.

He is the one that you spend the most time with. This mentor needs to be able to guide you through most of your programs, so he needs to have similar fields of work and play as you aspire to. This is the first one you want to report your AARs to, he will understand the most as he has had similar experiences. He may not be able to tell you what works, but he can tell you what won't work.

Also know that high-value men may not give this away for free. You will need to budget for this either in your financial plans or your time. Some may take acts of service as payment. Like running errands much like an assistant or intern. You will have to weight the cost to benefit of these cases. As most of these are short-term solutions. These Mentors will get you off the ground, dust you off, and give you a kick in the ass to get you moving again.

You may also gain some good information from internet forums. Which are for most purposes as close as you can get to a Men's Club today. Just be mindful that on the forums, not all is what it seems. You may be getting guidance from a complete tool. If there is a field report of a similar situation, you can try to replicate it and judge the results for yourself through your AAR.

You should continue to pick up books, all kinds of books, even though you don't agree with the message. It can be eye-opening to see what some of the mainstream thinkers are spewing. It is as close to a crystal ball as you can truly get. We recommend reading and studying all of those mentioned at the beginning of the book. Follow the rabbit hole they lead you down.

Not all of it will meet your needs, but that's fine not a big loss. Reading is keeping you from binge-watching TV anyway. Something that got you in this mess, to begin with.

Speaking of that, we advise you to stick to non-fiction, as fiction books are no better than sitting on the couch watching TV. You may enjoy the entertainment they provide, and that is fine in moderation. We are not telling you to stop something that you enjoy. You should just limit the amount of time and attention that you give them. Remember the reason you're currently at this stage in life is that you didn't put enough time into personal growth and sat on the couch too much. Speak life into your ideas, your goals, and yourself. This positive law of attraction is real. You will manifest the things that you focus on.

Think of the famous motivational speakers you have read about or watched videos of them speaking about growth. Now imagine they are found speaking about them feeling depressed, doubting themselves, or sad. You may never see this if they are smart due to it undermines their overall position of influence. Look for positive action to take! No matter how small or insignificant. The action, much like an investment in the stock market will provide compound interest in value. Stop complaining about anything!

You may discuss an issue of concern with a peer or a close friend, however, it must not be a one-dimensional conversation about you or your negative feelings!

Sharing AARs

Once you have filled a Board of Directors with men who are about a 50/50 split with higher-level men and lower-level men than you. You need to start sharing your AARs with them and getting honest feedback. The complete AAR Package includes your Filed Report and your initial AAR. You need to share it all. Don't be embarrassed.

If you fail to do this, your guidance will be skewed, and you will never run a fully improved plan. Wasting more of your time, and worse the time of these men who have volunteered to assist. You must be completely and brutally honest in the presentation. Don't hold back, throw it all on the table, you have nothing to hide from these men. Hell, you vetted them for this reason.

Present the package and wait for the knowledge to flow. There should be only one rule here, the only time you speak during this process is to ask clarifying questions. You are not to argue or get offended by their response. They are there to give you what you need not a pat on the head.

Listen to every word. If you have done your job correctly in the field report and AAR from the previous chapter (describing the situation honestly and accurately), they were there with you while you screwed this up and can tell you exactly where you went wrong.

They will even be able to tell you exactly what position you were in when you did it. Shut the Fuck Up (STFU), just listen and take notes. Very detailed notes. These men are showing you your blind spots, this is to help you. Accept the help and keep your emotions and ego in check. They will cloud your judgment to mistake truth for falsehood. You need to take notes because regardless of how hard you try, your fee fees may still get the better of you. You need to look back at your notes a couple of days later with a clear head. Reassess them and what your Board was telling you, they will probably make much more sense.

This is the reason for the only rule of asking clarifying questions. If you can't keep it together through this process, you may run off at the mouth. If that happens the Board will fire you and they will no longer be willing to assist. Hence the membership and vetting requirements of the Men's Clubs of old.

Once you have all your answers in your notes. Walk away from them for at least two hours and clear your head. Better yet go pray at the Iron Church. This will get you in the right mental frame. Then you can reengage with the complete package and work it into the current program.

When you have the complete package, reevaluate the goal and performance. Doing this will give you a chance to adjust your path. You may even need to completely change course. Understand that a course correct may be a real possibility. You may also need to put goals on hold and shoot for a lesser impact one to get some momentum, or to get a win during a dry spell.

All of this is perfectly fine. You are the one who must live your life. You get to set the standard and the timeline. Know that if your progress slows to a crawl while the rest of the Board is chugging along like a bullet train, you may be asked to leave the Board as the distance for you to catch up is too great. This is fine also. Just rework the process again to find a suitable board. The key is constant improvement, some people improve faster than others. It is not the end of the world. Just keep working on it.

The opposite side of the coin is true as well. If your Board has not improved at the rate that you have and you become the smartest man in the room. Then it is time to leave and rework the process again. Boards come and go; you can still respect them and grab a drink with them from time to time. They are still high-value men; they are just not on your caliber anymore.

The relationship between you and the Board is like any other. If you are more high value, then a demotion is in order. If they are too high value for you then you will be demoted. Are you starting to see the pattern yet?

Yes, we are telling you to treat all relationships as business transactions. And, yes, we mean all. The women in your life, the Board of Directors, your business partners. All of them. Treat them the same. The reason is that your emotional bullshit got you in a position to read a book from people you don't know to improve your life. Castrate the damn bull, so he will stop making other cows that you have to clean up after.

We are not advocating for you to become a complete emotionless robot; we are only advocating the emotions should not rule your judgment and decision-making process. That has been the point of this material thus far, fair warning it will continue to be this way.

All relationships are "give and take", at times there is more give than take. That is fine for short periods but can grow exhausting in the long term. If your current way of doing things were working, you would not be reading this book. Here is a free AAR for you, maybe your emotional attachments to certain relationships did not help you get here.

If you are truly doing all the heavy lifting for the Board, your job, the neighbor, your kids, or your wife. Maybe its time to use the nuclear option (more on this later). Although not ideal, it is not ideal to set yourself on fire because other people are cold either.

Are you starting to notice the theme and progression of the book yet? We explained what the standard is and why it is, we told you how to get there, and we explained how to check your results with the help of others. You should be doing the work and making actual progress in raising your SMV/RMV, Performance, and Frame. What comes next?

If you guessed a couple of bonus chapters to still salvage your relationships before, we go scorched earth, then you would be right. We are getting you to the point of being cold-hearted, not completely heartless. Calm down, high speed. You must truly try everything in the arsenal before we are willing to just chalk up half our shit to the nuclear option.

PARENTING – NATURE VS NURTURE

"Nature, to be commanded, must be obeyed."

-       Francis Bacon

Nature is traditionally associated with the feminine, i.e., Mother Nature. This is due to the fickleness, seemingly sporadic, and violence of the weather. Sounds like a few women we know. We argue that this is a carry-over to the time before modern science. A time before man possessed the knowledge to forecast the weather. We argue that it seems nature is more of the masculine sense. Nature sees a polluted beach, fuck it, send a hurricane to throw that shit around so the pissant humans will finally pick it up. Seems like what is known in the military as a "Brown Round Tornado".

This is when a Drill Sargent finds a private's wall locker unlocked and they fling everything inside it all over the place. Oh, no there is stuff on this bed that doesn't belong (even though the tornado put it there), that can't be, the bed is then moved, with extreme force. Well, now this bed is not in its place, it must be moved and toppled. Etc., etc., etc. et al. That seems more like "Father Nature" to us.

In a family dynamic, the father is more of the Nature aspect as we have argued Mother Nature has more masculine traits when taken into full account. Nature is more uncaring that what humans for the past gave her (him?) credit for. She is a firm believer in actions and consequences. She will hold all accountable for their stupidity. Doesn't that sound like a father to you?

In a traditional two-parent household, which we have already explained is best for all children, the father is the disciplinarian, and the mother is the caring, companionate one. The famous line from mothers everywhere when a kid gets in trouble, "Just wait until your father gets home" proves the point. Then the child waits for hours in absolute fear.

This is further engrained in children at a young age when they learn that the father is the source of rough housing, and the mothers are the source of kissing of "boo-boos" and band-aids for no reason. Fathers around the world loathe the frivolous use of band-aids when an open wound is not currently dripping (at a minimum) blood. Rub some dirt on it and walk it off.

The masculine is the natural state of the world, and the feminine is the unnatural state. Fathers are known for dishing out consequences and forcing lessons from mistakes. Mothers are known for hugging the pain away and making it all better. That is why if you see a child get hurt, they will run to Mom and only Dad if Mom is not present. They know that Dad will make them deal with the pain and not give two shits about the child's fragile feelings. Mom will make this big dramatic scene to show that she is taking care of her children, but Dad will just brush it off.

For example, David, as a little league baseball coach,

(if you want to lay down with single moms on the regular ,become a little league coach) when a kid got hurt, the contrast in the reaction was staggering. The Mom would jump up to the fence with a worried look on her face doing everything she cannot charge the field as parents were not allowed. He would give her a reassuring wave and go check on the player. He would ask first, "Are you hurt or are you injured?". The players knew that hurt was pain only and injured was pain with the immobility of an extremity.

When they answered hurt, he would pick up some dirt and sprinkle it on the ailment, then tell the player to "Rub that in and walk it off". Seconds later, the player would be miraculously healed and back to normal and ready to play ball. Bad Cop would return to the dugout as if nothing happened. But he could see out of the corner of his eye the relief on the player's mom's face. Do you know what happened seconds after that? Yup, it was a moist night as the hamster in Mom's head replayed the scenario over and over in her mind.

That said, masculine nature is equivalent to the real-world order of consequences and learning from mistakes. The masculine nature is that of evolution and natural selection. We have heard many male role models say after something stupid was done, "I bet you'll never do that again" and offer little more, letting the victim of their stupidity stew over their actions.

Females, on the other hand, will immediately start to provide comfort and say, "It's OK", even when it's not. They usually follow it up or say it concurrently with a hug, then they will proceed to fix the problem for the injured party. Males offer little help, as an important part of the learning process is picking up the pieces of your own mistakes.

Both aspects of nature and nurture are important for the growth and development of human beings. However, this has recently gone awry within most of the western civilization. The masculine aspects of nature have been trampled and the feminine aspects of nurture have been elevated. To be clear, we are indifferent to society doing this. However, the results can be easily seen.

Boys are forced to learn in a public school system that is operated by females. They are required to sit in class, be quiet, and behave. This forces them to act and learn as females would. The masculine class of metal, wood, and mechanical shop have been scrapped from most public schools. Boys who stand up for themselves and fight back against bad behavior targeted at them are suspended due to no-tolerance policies.

The public-school systems do not care if your head was shoved in a toilet, and you almost drowned, and to survive you had to kick your attacker in the crotch. You are just as guilty and will suffer the same consequence. Violence in any form is crucifiable, and young men are paying the initial price, as society is starting to pay the price now for years of these types of policies.

As men are no longer allowed to be men. Any display of masculinity in public is ridiculed and shamed as toxic.

Society is forcing young boys to learn in a feminine manner, behave in a feminine manner, and suppress the masculine that grows in them from the first day of puberty. Society is attempting to turn boys into horrible versions of girls and force them into college to continue the emasculation process. Until they can get married, and his wife can take care of him. All the while she bitches to her girlfriends about what a child he has become. Knowing little that society has conditioned him to be that way since birth. Caring even less that her lack of support is not helping her situation and that women of previous generations forced the environment that created him.

Society tells us men through public school systems, the college system, media, politics, and policies that we are the problem. Every father portrayed on TV is a bumbling idiot not even capable of the simplest of tasks. The best male role model you can find in a sitcom today is the present but completely absent father. He sits on the couch and only speaks one line an episode for comedic effect. He doesn't discipline his children or even acknowledges their presence. The family goes about their way of living their lives around him.

Any show that portrays masculinity in its proper form is an immediate success. Breaking Bad (once the main character turns full Heisenberg), most senior executives on Mad Men (once you understand the difference in Alpha and Beta behavior it is very clear and cringy), and most male characters on Yellowstone (the only Beta is the enemy of the show). More examples of covert communication at work.

Even still, online dating has created a world of such abundance for women that they have a false sense of value. Women with lower SMV can date men with much higher SMV because, in the online dating world, women are a hot commodity. A single woman can get thousands of men hitting on them and choose the best to get a free meal out of. These men are so desperate for attention that they will gladly bat in lower leagues because it's easy and they don't have to waste time running games in the wild.

Furthermore, a woman can post pictures of their half-naked body online and tens of thousands of Simps will throw validation her way in the form of likes and comments (translation, their time, and attention). Some even try to take it further and send DMs (Direct Messages) to these women expecting a shot. Additionally, some men now pay a monthly fee to see specific women naked on the internet. With the abundance of free porn, why would anyone pay to see just one specific woman? You have millions of women you can see doing anything you can imagine on a device in your hand for absolutely nothing.

This does not consider that the simple abundance of porn causes issues among men. If you have an unlimited supply of naked women willing to defile themselves in the palm of your hand, then you reduce the satisfaction from your partner. This does not consider the mental aspects of this availability and abundance.

33% of men report suffering from erectile dysfunction. Could this be due (or at least attributing) to the abundance of willing females to defile themselves online for a quick paycheck?

Today's man has lost his masculinity and his ability to be the unrelenting force of nature the world needs. Society has programed into men that their masculinity if it affects others in ways that they don't like is toxic.

The world and all societies on it need strong men, if for nothing else than to raise strong boys who become strong men. Strong men are needed to keep the world balanced.

We are no longer balanced as a society. There may be outliers in rural areas and some homes in major cities. But they are the exception that proves the need.

Society is attempting to turn young boys into lesser versions of girls. It is also turning women into lesser versions of men. Women are told to go to college, start a career, and freeze their eggs so that they can keep working. Some companies are making egg freezing and fertility treatments a part of their benefits packages to achieve this and keep women out of the home. Women are letting the biological clock run out and having a baby at 40 when the chances of birth defects and the risk of complications during birth are extremely high.

Men don't get a say in this. If a man wants to have a child with her at a younger age as it would make more sense to not attend his child's high school graduation on the brink of retirement. Her body, her choice. He has no choice but to deal with it, even though he is an "equal" partner in the relationship. She just wants to focus on her career right now, so tough shit Brian, no kids yet until she says so.

Once a man becomes a father, he has a set of totally different challenges. If he does what is natural for him to be the masculine nature aspect. If he does not control the frame of the relationship then he will have to hear from his wife that he is being mean, or worse yet, he is being abusive. There have been times when a wife has called Child Protective Services of her husband because he took slight corporal punishment on the child.

The father may have given his child two or three quick spanks on the ass and now he must deal with a full investigation to be determined by the state if he is fit to raise his children. Now, these spanks are not life-threatening, they didn't even leave a mark, but the father may only get supervised visitation in the future. All because he was attempting to instill some discipline in his children. This is society's attempting to wash natural selection, evolution, and all things masculine out of our DNA.

As a father, you must instill discipline in your children. You cannot count on any other adult to do it or even assist. You must be the nature aspect of the world. The teachers won't do it (most of them are female anyway and focus on nurturing), the coaches won't (they're not allowed), and your wife won't do it, it is all up to you. If you want better for your children than you had, which is truly the only wish for a father, then you will have to teach your sons how to be proper men and to step up when needed. You will also have to set an example for your daughters, you need to be the man that all other men in her life are measured against and found lacking.

The positive but tern example of a high valued man is your responsibility as a father to your children. The emotional stability of your household. How do you respond and treat your wife or girlfriend? The high valued man isn't truly a man unless he becomes proficiently consistent with being responsible for others. Some single mothers these days are babying their sons and setting them up for failure. Inadvertently turning them into the exact Beta male they wouldn't want now or previous, just to compensate for the guilt of a failed relationship or an absentee father. The female child will grow up with daddy issues and loose respect for themselves and their mother if single parenting exists in their upbringing.

To do this you must be the nature Ying to your wife's nurture Yang. There must be balance returned to the world. You must start in your household. It will probably not happen in your generation, maybe it can happen in your child's, but it will surely happen in your grandchild's generation. Only if we men do our jobs at home. So, get your fucking ass off the damn couch and get to work.

You must take the time to teach your sons masculine things. They should know how to fix things. They don't need to be able to build a house from the ground up, but they should know how to clean out a P-Trap, unclog a shower drain (it's going to be his wife's hair anyway), change the oil in a car, grill a steak to perfection, and keep a lawn green. Boys learn best by doing, male brains are just wired that way. Schools teach boys by having them sit still while a teacher lectures. This is how female brains learn best. Males need to get their hands dirty. They need to take things apart and figure out how they work. You must motivate this behavior in your sons. That is a natural way. A boy needs a tap on the head or two to keep the flashlight steady, it is a rite of passage.

Your daughters should also know at least; how to change a tire, check the oil and other fluid levels in a car, unclog a toilet, and shut the water off to a leaky faucet. She doesn't need to know how to repair them just stop further damage. Again, this is your job as the masculine nature. Let mom, teach them how to bake a cake, clean their clothes, and keep the house clean. Your job is to assist her with this to ensure your kids do these things to your standards. Mom teaches home economics, Dad teaches shop.

NOBODY CARES NO ONES COMING

Participation Trophies

In life, there are winners and losers. Not so much anymore in children's sports. Every kid gets a trophy just for showing up. There are no scores kept and everyone is a winner.

How are children supposed to know if what they are doing is working? The process of playing sports is like the Field Test and AAR process. You practice (train), play a game (field testing), coaches evaluate (AAR), and practice to correct mistakes from the last game (retraining), then play another game, (rinse and repeat). If you don't know if you won or not, what's the point, it's just a bunch of kids in a field throwing or kicking a ball around. Yay fun, but no learning or improvement is happening.

Competition is the natural order of things. Hell, you exist because you were the fastest swimmer of thousands of other swimmers. We were all created in the spirit of competition. Winners get to go home with some pride and say, "I will do what I did last time, only better", and bang the cheerleader at the after party. The losers get to face some minor adversity and say, "Back to the drawing board".

Real competitive sports are the best way to teach young children how to get over adversity. It needs to start when they are young, it teaches them resiliency. It also teaches them the AAR process, which they will use for the rest of their lives to get better at whatever they are doing.

It is a necessity. You will now have to be that for your children. You will have to point out mistakes and give advice on how to improve. You no longer have a choice; the options of sports have been taken off the table in most places. Your kids may get their first taste of this in High School sports. That is too late. It needs to be done at the little league and pee wee level. A coach does not want a whiny brat of a teenager who throws tantrums on the field, it's embarrassing and a display of his lack of leadership. Do him a favor and get your kids used to it early.

Another option is combat sports. The nonsense from other sports has not corrupted that area yet. There are still clearly defined winners and losers. In martial arts, there is a good deal of discipline, respect and tradition taught to young people. It may be something worth looking at to get some assistance in this aspect.

Make no mistake, if you take all of this on alone, you will appear to be the biggest asshole on the planet. Even to your wife, who will downplay and sabotage what you are trying to do. She will even blatantly do this in front of you. You will get evil eyes on every single occasion. And don't even think about getting any that night. It's completely out of the question.

Understand, there are real-life consequences for not instilling resilience in your children. They are growing up in a world that is full of danger and dangerous people. If they don't have resilience, they will not be able to process the situation and think their way out of it. They will just be stuck in an endless loop of OMG. This process is referred to as the OODA (Observe, Orientate, Decide, Act) Loop, look it up. A person stuck on the endless loop of OMG is stuck on step 1 of this loop, it will cost them dearly if they can't break it.

Teaching them resilience is simple, acknowledge their

feelings and move on. "I know it sucks to lose, but...". This is where you throw in the Field Report. "But you were not setting your rear foot on the mound as coach taught you", now that you have addressed the needs improvement portion, we move on to retraining. "You and I will work on this in a couple of days", you are motivating them to keep working, and rewarding them with your time and attention. This shows that you value hard work, it also gives them a couple of days to get over the fee fees. Now, is just the rinse and repeat portion of the process.

Parenting is not an easy task; it has plenty of challenges. The challenges get bigger if you do not keep your frame in the relationship with your wife. You must build trust in her and your kids by being engaged in all of them. You can't be a good husband and a great father sitting on the couch shoving shredded cheese from the bag in your mouth.

You must do what is necessary for your children. And raising them to know what needs to be known and that bad choices have consequences. It is going to be a hard job. A very hard one, but a necessary one. A job made for a high-value man. So, Own Your Shit.

CAPTAIN (CPT) AND FIRST OFFICER (FO) MODEL

If you have done all the hard work of vetting the right woman, married her, and started to build a life together, now is not the time to rest. You need to keep the frame or get it back if you lost it. Even though she may be your wife for a couple of years now, she is still going to shit test you. If you now have children, they are going to shit test you, and she is going to shit test you on how you respond to their shit tests.

When you get back the frame (or never lost it, you beast of a man), then the relationship should automatically fall into the CPT/FO model. Your frame and her submission will get you to this automatically. It is the advised model to follow to ensure the frame is maintained and all family members get what they need to be productive adults. You know, an upstanding pillar of the community.

This model appears to the untrained eye that the patriarchy (there is that bad word again) is in full control of your household. However, it is your frame that has carried over to your wife and she has given full submission and follows your leadership to the end.

Your kids have submitted as well as they have realized

that "Father Knows Best". You have demonstrated time and time again that your guidance has been the best for all.

You constantly pass your kids' and wife's shit test, you support your wife when she needs it, and your kids get everything you can give them (when needed). You defend them at school when they are forced to defend themselves or others incapable of defending themselves. They walk into the house from school and get to work on the homework because they know the standard and get it done without a word.

That is the pinnacle of the frame. You no longer must maintain a frame with the day-to-day, the family does it on their own. You only must get involved with the slightest of infractions when the family just leans against the wall of your boundaries or break the speed limit of your standards. They do it themselves and don't need your help any longer.

Those on the outside of this relationship would think that the man is controlling and abusive. However, he is just giving his masculine energy to the rest of the family. The ones who receive this benefit could not be happier, to follow his lead, and give two shits what others think. They gain all the benefits from his knowledge, wisdom, experience, and leadership. The wife is happy, the kids are happy, and he can focus on his plan, which makes him happy.

The CPT can steer the ship (yes, the relationship) as he sees fit based on the needs of his plan.

The FO handles the rest. The house, the meals, the basic needs of the kids, and she is happy to do so. Only because he is at the peak of his performance. Not only, his peak with her, but the kids. They have also followed his lead and are striving with his leadership.

If you are currently not in the above type of household. You have some work to do. You cannot, we repeat, cannot force your wife and kids to fall in line just because you say so. This will end badly for you. You must Raise your SMV/RMV, Performance, and Frame first. Your positive outcomes need to be almost constant with an ever-increasing impact on your household. You must fix your self first, lead by example and they will want to hop on the train wherever you take them.

Get a purpose, plan, and run it, like a fucking CPT. Your wife will be the first to jump on board. This is best as you will need her to be the FO. Slowly the kids will get on the train as they see you and your wife barreling to better things. Everyone wants better things; they just don't want to do the work to get them. To be honest, you have been giving your kids better and better things for no reason. Again, stop rewarding unsatisfactory behavior and performance. Your job doesn't do it, why the fuck do you.

Your wife being on board is a necessity for you to succeed. She will be the one micromanaging the household. Yes, we know this sounds "degrading" for her and "misogynistic" for you. We can assure you that it is not, it's just your social conditioning talking.

In 2004 a study was conducted in the Netherlands that found female doctoral students viewed as not being as committed to their work as the male students by all participants regardless of gender. Another study in Italy found the same results. In 1973 at the University of Michigan, psychologists found that women in supervisory roles adopted more masculine traits and coined the term, Queen Bee Syndrome. Another study at the University of Toronto expanded on the previous study by finding that women overwhelmingly prefer to work for a male supervisor as they find it less stressful.

More covert communication from the female stands, boys. Your wife is comforted by your leadership once you have demonstrated you deserve to be followed. She prefers it, your frame is her happy place. It is on the couch, wrapped in a warm blanket, sipping hot tea while she binges on her favorite show on a lazy Sunday afternoon.

She will happily clean the house, get the kids off to school, keep your underwear clean, and give you a hot meal when you walk in the door if you are worthy of these things. She does not reward bad behavior either. Your reward for good behavior is a doting wife who will do anything for you when you ask, yes, we mean ANYTHING.

She will only be your FO if you are her CPT. You can't be an entry-level deckhand and expect her to treat you like royalty. You must bring your fucking A Game every waking minute of every day until they lay your cold dead body in the ground if you expect to reap the benefits of being a CPT.

Once you raise your overall value, then you can start gaining control of the wheel back from her. She will buck and shit test you, you know how to pass them. It's not her fault, you were a sad sack of shit until recently. She has lost some faith in you. Play the long game and get the wheel back. Stay on your course, it will improve over time. Remember that you did not become a piece of shit overnight, it will take months if not years before you reach a sustainable level of submission from your FO.

She knows how to be an FO; she just needs a CPT who has proven the worthiness of her submission. Once you gain the submission (that you probably had but lost) she will just need to be reminded of your standards. When that happens, it will be a night and day difference. You will know when she gives it (back) to you.

I'm sure she showed you plenty of FO behavior in the early stages. She probably made you plenty of dinners, so many that you have packed on plenty of pounds. She has made your life so comfortable by doing your laundry, making your meals, doing the grocery shopping, picking up your dry cleaning, dropping your kids off a school, and all the other day-to-day that needs to be done.

How did you repay her devotion? By sitting on your fat ass until you forgot what your penis looks like. Letting the kids get away with murder and still get the latest iPhone because you got tired of them whining about it. You stopped dating her and giving her a break from the mother and wife duties, not even for a two-hour dinner where she can get out of her yoga pants and have a reason to put on a dress.

We are not advocating for all this just because. Even worse when you both need her to work and do all the household things that need getting done while you sit on the couch.

Once you start getting your shit together, she will follow suit. When you start dropping the weight, you don't have to tell her anything, she will notice and start picking it up. When you start dressing better, she will start dressing better. You need to reward the good behavior that she displays. She is rewarding your hard work with her adjustments. Covert communication, remember.

Stop running your mouth and run your plan. She will see the results and appreciate it, then start stepping her game up. Why? Because you're no longer a bag of assholes. You are now a man getting back in the game, and she wants to keep up with you. She married you for a reason all those years ago, and now you are getting back to that best version of yourself.

She will just start doing the things that she used to do. Yes, even including all that nasty stuff she used to do to you in college. Yes, we are telling you that when you start busting your ass again, she will start doing the same. It's that simple. Stop being lazy and act with a fucking purpose. Raise your SMV/RMV, increase your performance, and maintain your frame. Outcomes and impacts are what she cares about. Stop sitting on your ass and wasting your time and attention on dumb shit that doesn't matter.

Women want to provide comfort it is their biological makeup. Remember the Nature vs. Nurture chapter. They are driven to do so. You must make yourself worth her comfort providing. She will do anything you need without hesitation if you are living your purpose.

She will stop nagging if you just do the shit that needs to be done. If you don't know how to fix it, learn how. You live in an age where anything can be found online, or the just take your ass to the hardware store. Most employees

GOOD COP BAD COP

of those stores will be able to help you figure it out. If you can't learn it, then pay a handyman to fix it.

Don't get her to make the appointment and sit with him while he fixes it. You make the appointment; you watch his ass fix it. This way you will learn how to fix it in the future. Just as your son will learn how to change his oil. It's the same concept, you just won't get smacked on the head as many times.

You are also leading by example. Your kids are watching you ask for help, gain knowledge, and get your hands dirty. They, especially your son, will learn by watching you learn.

By being the one who takes responsibility, you are also preventing another man who has a masculine skill alone in your house with your family. This will prevent any straying if you are still not to the level of SMV/RMV that you should be.

You must be a CPT. You must take responsibility for all things in your household. You must set the standard and boundaries. You must live up to them first before anyone else will. The only way you will get the best FO is to be the best CPT. You do this by owning your shit.

NUCLEAR OPTION

We hardly ever recommend hitting the red button, as this ensures mutual destruction. But, sometimes, in rare cases, it is necessary. If you are married then the nuclear option will change your, your wife's, and your kid's lives forever.

Know that you will probably be divorced raped by the state for half your stuff, alimony (in some cases, for life regardless of if she remarries), and child support. Also know that you will also have to pay half of any cost associated with the kid's medical, dental, and extracurricular activities.

If you don't, you will be incarcerated. In the US, the only debtor prison that still exists is the family court system. That doesn't even consider the time with your kids that you will miss, as most judges grant majority custody to mothers.

You will lose valuable time with a son that needs a good masculine male role model. Your daughter needs one as well. You also run the risk of not being aware of the men that your ex-wife will have in your kids' life.

This can have devastating effects on your relationship with your kids. A relationship that is already strained due to separate households and conflicting schedules, standards, and boundaries.

Know for a fact, if you hit that red button, you will not be divorcing the woman that you married. Most women become completely heartless during the divorce process. She will drag it on for a coffee cup, just because it means something to you. That is the only reason she is doing it; you get nothing, and you will like it.

A divorce can drag on for years, and the court system is happy to allow it. Every minute that you spend dealing with it is more money for attorneys. Every new filling is a new fee that needs to be paid. Every time you get a raise, your ex-wife can take you back to court and ask for more until your youngest kid turns 18.

She can withhold visitation, and you must take her back to court generating more income for the attorneys and family court. You can call the police, but they can't do anything about it as family law is a civil matter and not a criminal one.

The family court is a bureaucracy that depends on itself for its survival. You need to know the risks in your environment as judges' interpretation of laws and situations vary widely. A local attorney in the area should be consulted before any decisions are made on the use of the nuclear option.

You must be at your complete breaking point. You must have done all that you can to raise your SMV/RMV to its complete best. You have demonstrated, over the years that you reliably produce positive outcomes with high impact.

The real issue in a relationship and the use of the nuclear option is the lack of frame. Since "No Fault Divorce" laws have become the norm for most western societies, there is a chance that she may file on you. In 2005, the American Sociological Association conducted a research study to find which person is responsible for initiating a divorce. They found that in nearly 70% of cases, women initiated the divorce process.

However, the option is there, if you must use it, act and get a divorce. Get a lawyer and protect your rights as a father! Ultimately, your peace of mind and happiness are more important in the long run. Staying for the kids is a terrible idea. All your going to show them is how not to love someone or properly be loved themselves. It's inevitable and can't be hidden from their awareness.

The high divorce rate may be due to men no longer maintaining their SMV/RMV, having stopped performing, and lost frame. Most marriages that stand the test of time in the past, were able to do so because the men at least maintained their value throughout the marriage.

If she is nagging you constantly, your bedroom is only a room to sleep, and you just sit around the house doing nothing but drinking and watching the game. This reality may be closer than you realize. You need to get your shit together now.

All the nagging and lack of sex is another covert communication that she does not desire you anymore. You have become a sack of shit over the years, and nobody wants to be with that. You also must remember that she can easily go find Chad McHorsecock on Tinder and be in the throws of his meat within the hour.

All men are pigs, there is always somebody willing to throw a bone at your wife. It doesn't matter what she looks like. If you know she has thrown on an extra 50 pounds after the second kid, it doesn't matter to the random dude down the street.

He gets all the benefits that you stopped getting for nothing. That's the way it goes if you can't get it together. So, you better start now.

Aggressive Posturing

When nuclear countries are trying to bang on their chest like a gorilla as a show of dominance, they will start testing their nuclear program's capabilities. Most of the time, it is done publicly. This is known as aggressive posturing.

The same can be a warning sign in a relationship. It is all done through covert communication. She is picking up on your improvement and wants to join in. Great, you're gaining frame. She is following your lead and bettering herself.

The flip side to this is if she doesn't even try to get better. This is equivalent to the US not even wasting the time to notice that North Korea now has nukes. It is her telling you that she has no faith in your follow-through, and you won't do shit.

At the early stages of your plan, this is fine. She will get on board when you start showing some consistency. And the benefits of the FO should be back in full swing. Great, that's what you wanted. Close the football (the briefcase that houses the nuclear launch codes) and give it back to the Agent. There will be no mushroom cloud today.

If you have run the plan for a couple of years, and you are now a much better man than you were when she married you and she still has done nothing. You need to readdress the frame and AAR more interactions with her.

Are you passing the Shit Tests? Are you even getting Comfort Tests anymore?

If you're not getting Comfort Tests, she may be thinking of making the first launch. She may already have an exit strategy and is just waiting for the last few ducks to line up. Or you are just giving her enough comfort with your day-to-day, treating her like the center of the universe.

Which means you are not paying attention to what this material is telling you. You are trying to get fantastic results with only half the work. Women don't work that way. They want it all in a high-value man.

If you can't get her submission, then it is only a matter of time before she leaves you or starts banging the neighbor every week. You need to go back and readdress the Frame Chapter. Start passing shit tests and run YOUR plan. Stop running HER plan.

If you still have not seen improvement once your SMV/RMV and performance are up, and still there is no change in her behavior after a couple of years of running your plan. You have a couple of choices. You can just wait it out in a sexless marriage, you can just get yours any way you can (this involves cheating, which will end in the nuclear option anyway because you will get caught, so not recommended), or hit the red button and get it over with.

Preparing for Launch

If you have decided to go ahead and hit the red button, you need to do some preparation first. All this needs to be done in consultation with a local attorney who is aware of the laws and family court environment. This will probably not go according to your plan, but you may be happier in the long run by doing so.

Step one is to get that attorney and find out if your prenuptial agreement is enforceable in your state. Prenuptial agreements are highly recommended months before the wedding. Even if you are moving in with a girlfriend, you need an attorney to draft an agreement before the move-in date. All these documents are binding in most jurisdictions.

If your prenup is unenforceable, then a postnuptial may be in order. The postnuptial should reinforce the prenup and account for any changes since the marriage began, i.e., additional children, major purchases, and sentimental items that were gained during the marriage.

Prenup and postnuptial agreements are usually enforceable within five years in most jurisdictions. If you do not have a prenup or it is past the five-year mark, it does not hurt to get postnuptial at the beginning of getting your shit together.

It is in your best interest to never combine debts, bank accounts, leases, or mortgages during the marriage. Your car needs to be in your name only and her car needs to be in her name only. If you did combine any of these things, the postnuptial needs to address those things. It is also not wise to leave the family home. If the situation is unsafe, however, it may be necessary to stay on this side of a cell, the air is cleaner out here.

If you're soon to be ex-Mrs. is not violent, then stick it out. This also needs to be covered with legal advice. Your attorney should be able to get all the legal jargon

NOBODY CARES NO ONES COMING

in the document to this effect that will be enforceable. Remember, family law is under the umbrella of civil law. It is no different than a contract.

Where the line is crossed, is when one spouse breaks a criminal law. Once that happens, the agreement is void. Do not under any circumstances get baited into arguments or allow things to get physical during the prep and launch phase, just walk away. Women have been known to make false police reports.

You should assume that anything done in her or your kid's presence will be exaggerated and reported to the courts. If you could not get the frame back before this phase. You should not give a shit about anything that she does at this point. Just let her do her thing and you do yours. Maintain an active role in your kid's life as if you start to separate from them and disconnect, nor doing this will hurt you in family court when it comes to custody.

You should be striving for a total of 50/50 shared custody of your kids. Maintaining a healthy active role in their lives will assist in this process.

If you are sharing finances, start the separation of accounts during this phase. Of course, your attorney will advise if this is a good idea or not. Know that women have been known to empty shared bank accounts on their way out of a marriage or relationship. You will never see this money again and there is nothing you can do to recover it. It is joint property. That is why you never combine them in the first place.

Additionally, you don't need to be making any big purchases now, so get your credit locked. An ex-wife of

Jason's ran up a ton of debt in his name, from predatory lenders on her way out the door. Lock your fucking credit now, all that she needs is your social security number and she can put any kind of debt on you that she wants.

You should not be changing anything about your lifestyle but running your plan. No new cars, no new boats, no new debt at all. Lock your credit and monitor it regularly.

Get your attorney to draw up the divorce papers but do not file them. Keep a copy in a safe place where she can't find them. Get a safe deposit box at a local bank or keep them in your office. DO NOT keep the divorce papers in the house. Keep them totally out of her reach.

You will need the element of surprise later. If she has seen them or knows you have an attorney, you're fucked. You are only doing this as a failsafe. If she finds out, it turns into a first strike. Hopefully, all this time and money preparing to launch is a waste.

We are still attempting to keep the marriage together at this point. We are just getting the ducks in a row just in case she dies on the hill of her frame. You will remain married to her if the frame is back in your control, and she submits and starts being the FO that you need.

Slapping the Big Red Button

If you have done everything to get the frame and still no improvement. And you have done all the preparation work in the prelaunch phase. You must be sure that there is nothing else you could have done, and the marriage is over, there is no going back once this step is initiated.

You will not be able to put this genie back in the bottle. Once you make the first move, you must see it to the end.

The fastest way through hell is to go straight through it. This is the final step before mutual destruction. Hold on, because this is going to be a very bumpy ride for you, at the very least for the next few months (if you did all the prep work), or years (if not).

This process is quite possibly going to be the ugliest months or years of your life. It is also going to be very detrimental to your kids. Especially, if you're soon to be ex-wife talks trash about you to them. Just assume that everyone in the household is going to turn on you.

There is no need in trying to defend yourself against this or attempt to stop it. This will only create situations where an argument can take place and you are not getting into arguments anymore. You are now beyond talking.

Once you have all the prep work done. It is time to create the ultimatum. These are based on the specific situation your household is in and the current state of your wife and where you need her to be.

If you need your wife to quit smoking, you need to get pamphlets, nicotine gum, and some nicotine patches. If you need her to lose some weight, get her a gym membership pamphlet from multiple gyms in the area. If you need her to clean the house, get a mop bucket and fill it with cleaning supplies. A month's worth of receipts or online order boxes. The list can be tailored to your needs, but it needs to be a visual representation of your needs.

Once you have all you need for the visual representation, you will need to get a copy (never the original) of the divorce papers that your attorney drew up from their hiding spot (with your signature already on them). You also need to block out some time (at least a couple of hours) when you and your wife can be alone.

Find a neighbor or a babysitter for the kids that can leave you and the wife alone in the home while you two discuss the situation. Your kids do not need to see what this conversation is going to turn into. It will also allow your wife to save face if she decided to get on the train you're driving. The kids should not be any the wiser if your wife decides to stay.

Now, the MAIN EVENT. Yes, this is the main event. She will react one of two ways, completely indifferent or a hysterical mess with the ugliest of crying imaginable. This is the reason for the privacy, you are giving one last chance to get her on board, or you walk away from the marriage and take all the benefits with you.

You will request a talk and have your visual aids ready. It is a simple talk from your perspective. A few sentences and that is all. Then provide the choice and sit back and stay calm. If you had a hard time earlier, now is not the time to do anything other than STFU. No more words from you until you get an answer.

You can simply start the conversation with; "I have been working to make things better for you and the kids for the last couple of years. I have had some success and I need your assistance to keep making them better. I need you to (start cleaning more, get healthy with me, stop spending so much money on needless things, or whatever you need in the form of support), and I need this done in 90 days. If you can't or won't then I have no choice but to go my separate way."

Your request needs to be a single thing that she can accomplish in a matter of months, preferably within 90 days. You need to make it doable, and the single most important thing. The rest of the issues can be worked out once you regain the frame. Remember, you are only attempting to regain the frame. You are not trying to completely fix years in 90 days.

Start with something that she can do alone. Nothing that needs to be done together. This is key, this needs to be solely her problem to fix. You can't give yourself up as an excuse if you fail to do your part.

This needs to be understood by you, "Start having more sex with me", is not a good need to hang your marriage on. It will fail, you should just hit that button and file without the conversation. You cannot, we repeat, cannot force intimacy. If you go this route, she will resent you for the rest of her life, even long after you are dead. DO NOT make this the stipulation.

Raising your SMV is the only way to increase intimacy in a marriage. Threatening divorce will not get this for you long term. Your marriage will end as if she signs the papers right there at the table that day. It may take a couple of years or until the kids leave the house, but make no mistake, your marriage is now over. Don't kill it over sex.

Her eyes will dart between the visual representations, there is no need to point them out. She is in an extreme emotional state, she's not stupid or blind. She knows what they mean. Your simple words were all the clarification she needed. No need to go into an evil villain monologue, just speak the simple sentences and wait (while you STFU).

Now one of the two reactions mentioned earlier will

happen. If she is cold and unmoved, then you will never get submission and she will die on that hill. That is all the answer you need. Do not be surprised when her hand reaches for the papers. Just STFU and answer any questions with "I suggest you have an attorney look at those".

Then be at the courthouse when they open to file. Get the clock started. SAY NOTHING MORE.

If you get all hell has broken lose emotional reaction, there is a chance your marriage can be saved. Even though she has some work to do, and you will have to maintain standards, she will try on her part. She will understand what you have been trying to communicate to her covertly over the last couple of years. This is just the overt communication that is the last straw. She understands because she would do the same thing if the roles were reversed.

Once the main event has begun it can take hours for her to come back down. All her range of negative emotions is going to hit her in the next couple of hours. Yes, all of them; anger, sadness, grief, worry. The dread level has just been sent through the roof. The hamster is about to run the wheel right off the stand. It will be ugly; we are talking full-blown running mascara to the cleavage ugly.

As ugly as it is, it is a good sign that she will give it her all. She will come to grips that this is the last straw. Or you have been a complete tool in the past and have given an ultimatum before and backed out. In which case this one will be no different. If you get an opening act, but not the main event. You're fucked. You played this card too many times. You probably won't see improvement; she is just saying whatever will get you to leave her alone. Once the main event is done start counting the days. Do not nag or bug her about it, don't even speak about it, just watch and count the days. If she wants to bring it up, just answer with "You know my thoughts on the matter", and that is all. You two already talked. A task was given, a standard was set, and a deadline to complete it. Don't waste any more of your time with this. Just continue to work on the plan like you have been doing for the last couple of years.

If she gets it done then great, move on to the next issue. Have the next issue, don't just let your marriage come down to a single straw. Have a plan to address all the issues. Mold her to the FO you need.

You don't need to brief her on the whole plan. Just give her a couple more things to take care of. When those are complete, then a couple more. You may have to micromanage in the initial stages but less as she progresses.

It will be key to maintain standards during this rebuilding process. You just gained the frame in one action, don't give it up slowly over time. That nonsense brought you to this point of opening the football and putting your finger on the button. Maintain the ground you gained and work for a little more each day.

If after 90 days, she has not completed your simple task or has not completed it to your standard. If it is the latter, then, you should have been pointing that out in the process and given her time to correct it. Again, go back to the Shit Test chapter. Point out the mistake in one sentence and walk away, no argument. You cannot falter on this point at this stage.

Your marriage is still on the brink, the football is still open, and she knows it. She can still be baiting you into an argument or altercation. It could be her pushing her red button.

It may be the only option she has. She can still set the relationship on fire with a mushroom cloud. It will look different than yours, the footballs are made by different contractors. She won't file or get an attorney; she will call your family court and raise your criminal court through domestic violence charges. Be wary of the possibility, it may be a long shot, just know it exists and act accordingly.

<u>Fire and Forget</u>

If you get no reaction, or the task is not met to standard, or the deadline has not been met. Then it is time to skin this pig, fire the fucking missile. Get on the phone with your attorney and get the rundown of the next step and an overview of the process you will be going through. If he or she tells you to file, start at the courthouse before getting off the phone. And follow ALL their advice to a T. Do not stray and do not assume. Get clarification from them as you need it before you take any further action.

It is extremely important to speak to her as little as possible. NEVER react to her emotions, you need to be completely heartless during this process towards her. Cold-hearted is not enough anymore. If you can't control your emotions; then leave, go for a walk, go pray at the iron church, go do anything productive. You cannot afford a mistake now.

You need to be involved in your kids' lives as much as possible after the button is pushed. They need your calm wisdom now more than ever. You do not get to talk shit or let them talk shit about her. All you need to say is "I know how you are feeling, we are all feeling the same way". This lets them know that you understand, but you are not going to act on the negative emotions.

Again, now is the time for stoicism more than ever. You need to control your emotions. When you are in private all alone without a single soul within miles, can you let that shit out? Don't even speak about it the situation to mutual friends. Not even the buddy whose wife is friends with your soon-to-be ex-wife. That shit will get back to her, it will be exaggerated, and dug up in court. This will make it harder for your attorney to get the papers approved, costing you even more money and dragging the process out even further.

Once you have walked through hell. Take stock. You surely need to run the AAR process on this one. It needs to be the most absolute AAR you have ever completed as this thing has the highest cost you will ever pay. You need to run the AAR from the moment you met her through today. Notice all those red flags you ignored.

Run the After-Action by the Board of Directors and follow the process. Adjust your boundaries and standards as needed to prevent this outcome again. Keep running the plan to your purpose.

You create your purpose outside of a single person for this scenario. If you still have your purpose, you still have a reason to continue working on your plan.

You still have your reason to get up in the morning. You still have the motivation to increase your gravitational pull. You will need and want it more than ever now.

GOOD COP BAD COP

On the positive side, even though it didn't work out, you are now a high-value man, and in high demand in all aspects of your life. You bad ass mother fucker, you.

There is life after divorce. You can start over again! You may be at the point where a sustained relationship with a woman isn't the requirement any longer. Johnathan is 50-year-old and has a second marriage that is not working out once again. The SMV/RMV/JMV have all gone down and his current marriage is not much better than the last, she's just a better person than the first ex-wife. He has all the tools and experience from the first marriage and lessons learned. Now, who's at fault? Get off your ass and make the necessary changes you know you are required to make! Or you can explore the final option in RMV which is leaving RMV behind for good! Lots of men are in this situation and are fine with it! If your 50 plus years old, find yourself alone, the kids are grown up, then we focus on the final chapter of ourselves.

Explore Late Bachelorhood

This time can be a very peaceful and fruitful chapter in your life. Maximize the JMV/SMV and enjoy your late bachelorhood. You have the life you wanted with the house and the vehicles if the divorces didn't force them to be sold off and you have your family and friends. Sex for you will occur when you want and we don't have to assist in this area, you can figure it out. Enjoy your freedom and safeguard your health.

It's ok to be alone and if you want company, well there is always a woman looking for a good man to spend time with. Dating over fifty apps are prevalent, and you are still a high-value man, especially now when most young guys are not confident or getting the job done. You have resources at your disposal, use them.

This is where the tables have truly turned. You keep getting older and the ladies stay the same age. Sugar daddies are happy, they don't have RMV issues, they enjoy the pleasures of young women and live happily, enjoying the freedom of not needing a relationship or a wife to define their lives. Have a meaningful relationship with your kids. Be a part of their children's lives, and fully embrace the life of late bachelorhood.

THE SPOILS OF WAR

"To the victor belong the spoils. In war or other contests, the winner gets the booty."

- Senator William Learned Marcy (1786-1857) of New York, credited 1832

Whether you are running your plan making gains, or you just survived a divorce, you are at war. You are at war with yourself. The stupid son of a bitch who talked you into sitting on the couch and letting your life go to shit is you. You have been in a constant struggle with yourself. It can be very tiring.

However, it is worth it. You get out of the process what you put into it. If you half-ass the work, you will get half-ass results. The only finish line is the grave.

You need to raise your SMV by dressing better, getting the golden ratio, and regularly grooming yourself better. You need to work at raising your leadership capabilities through books and experience. You must demonstrate your masculinity.

You will also be raising your RMV by having the appearance of someone who can protect, you will concurrently be raising the capability to do so by training in a combat sport. You need to raise your ability to provide by mastering your craft and running a side hustle. Your ability to preside will grow along with your ability to lead and your stoicism.

You have found a new (or renewed) purpose that motivates you to no end. This has led you to create plans that follow this purpose. You create field reports and AARs for all your activities to include personal, business, relationships, and parenthood. You have formed a trusted Board of Directors that helps and mentors you through the improvement process.

You focus your plans on ensuring positive outcomes with increasingly high impacts. All while maintaining a frame in your marriage or romantic relationships. You are now a complete stud, with a large gravitational pull. You are at the pinnacle of the masculine man. Women want you and men want to hang out with you.

What now?

Well, that is dependent on your situation. If you are still in a marriage, great. If you're not, great. If you are just running through your contacts list, tapping a different hook-up seven days a week, great. You get to decide what to do with your newfound greatness.

What does matter is your ability to be completely independent of outcomes that require other people?

Build some redundancy into your plans so if one fails, the other can swoop in and save the day.

The only person you can truly count on in this world will be you. You must plan accordingly. Whatever path you took to get here, be glad you made it this far. Take some time to enjoy what you have and be grateful for the hard work that got you here.

Do whatever you wish, you have won the battle, get some spoils. Use caution in doing this so that you do not take it too far. In the world of abundance, that we live in, it is quite easy to fall back on the couch with your bag full of chips and never get back up. Any reward in moderation.

You have earned the spoils of great sacrifice and grief. You are hopefully making more money than you ever have before; your kids are well-behaved and prospering, and your wife is functioning as a high-value woman.

If you no longer have a wife. Bask in the prospect of being a new high-value man in high demand with his pick of the litter. Use caution now and follow the newly adjusted standards and boundaries set by the divorce AAR. You should not even be considering another relationship for at least another year or ever.

Take that time to recover from the nuclear war and ensure your kids are doing ok with the new environment. No promotions above hookup or Plate for 12 months. No need to needlessly complicate your life yet. Just live it up.

If your wife worked through the process with you, congrats. You now have a fantastic wife. She is probably more into you now than when you first married. Take it all in. Appreciate what got you both there.

Now, get even further out of your comfort zone. Yes, we know it was hard. But it worked before, didn't it? But did you die? Not at all, you are now probably happier than you could have ever imagined possible. So, push a little more.

If you now have everything you could have ever wanted, you lack sufficient imagination. Come up with something else, there is a whole world out there. Get creative and do something people would say you would never do.

Just do something because you now can. Take an expensive vacation, buy a motorcycle, and take some calculated risks. Get out there and just live your life as you see fit.

No more fucks given to social conditioning telling you, "You can't do that", "that's awful", or "you shouldn't do that". Just do you, live it up.

If you find yourself single again (or were single the whole time), run a game on every attractive woman that you see, use caution at work, however. Don't shit where you eat. Yes, even run a game on that 10 that you think is out of your league. You should have enough confidence in yourself and your ability to perform that you no longer see women as in or out of your league. You can always use more buddies and plates.

If you are still married and your wife has become the FO that you need then enjoy the ride with her. Bring her into some new hobbies of yours. However, always have your own for just the boys. You don't want to fall into the same cycle that you did that put you in the shit place that was your marriage.

Remember, that you must continue to perform in this new state. If you don't, things will go back to what drove you to read this material in the first place. Then you have another set of problems. What worked this time will not work again.

The ultimatum strategy is a single use scorched earth process. It will not have the same effect the second or third time. If you are so bold as to attempt to use it a fourth time, it will have no effect. Now you're just the dumb fuck who cried wolf.

Once you get to the point of being high value, you cannot relapse and expect the same results. That mindset is what caused you to get to the place you were when you started. You will still be shit tested, you will still be comfort tested, and you will still need to display high value. You can enjoy the spoils of war on occasion. You cannot be a lazy sack of shit anymore.

You can stop if the work is too hard. But know that you will be right back where you started. Your life will return to the suck fest that it used to be. You must earn the happiness that you want. Nobody is going to hand that shit to you. Once you earn it, it must be maintained. Time will eventually kill all things. They will die faster if neglected. The grass is always greener where you water it.

CONCLUSION

You have read this material because you needed to know that you are the reason the things in your life keep happening to you. Everything that has happened to you since you were capable of conscious thought has happened because you decided to do a thing, be in a place, be with a person. You continued to make the same type of decisions and expected that one day you would wake up and it will just miraculously fix itself. All while you get to keep doing dumb shit.

You need to own all of it. Own that you packed on the pounds. Own that you can't get a promotion at work. Own that your wife can barely stand to touch you. Own that your kids don't respect you. Own every drop of the shit you put yourself into.

If you don't, you won't do anything to change it. You will just make excuses and continue to live your fantastically fucked life until the day you stop breathing. This is no way to live.

You have the power to change everything. You need to take responsibility for it. It is all your fault. We will say it again for those still fighting it, IT IS ALL YOUR FAULT.

Are you over your pity party yet? Good now get to work. Bust your ass to lose the weight. Bust your ass to fix your marriage. Bust your ass to get a promotion or get the hell out of there and to a place that will pay you more.

Just start busting your ass. Live your life to your purpose. If you make plans based on that purpose, then you will be motivated to continue to bust your ass. At the least, you will maintain what you gained and not backslide.

Fix your marriage that you fucked up. Raise that SMV and RMV by doing the work. Both of you will benefit from it. Practice some damn leadership in your household by owning all the shit. Own yours, your wife's, and your kids'. Own it all. Now you can fix that too.

After-Action everything you do. If you don't, you won't know what works and what doesn't. Review the results with a well-vetted Board of Directors, they will be able to show you the blind spots. They will also get you past some of your deepest challenges and guide you to the best outcome.

Always remember that no one cares how you feel about anything. The only thing that matters to others is the outcome and impact of your actions. Strive for a majority positive outcome and high-impact contributions. If you start getting negative outcomes, own that shit and correct it. If the impacts of your positive outcomes are low value, own that shit too. Think bigger and get creative to raise the impact.

You are the only one in control of your life. So, start acting like it. Stop putting your issues on the shoulders of others and expect them to fix them for you. Do the damn work.

Keep in mind that the strategies covered will work for all relationships. Yes, all of them. Your personal and professional ones. Everyone will Shit and Comfort Test you. Your boss, your coworkers, the waitress, the gas station clerk, everyone. The responses you give in your relationships will work with all the rest.

The mindset is what matters. If your coworkers don't do things to your standard, then address them with a single sentence and walk away. If your boss crosses a boundary, address it with a single sentence and walk away. Stop giving fucks to things that don't deserve them.

There is no reward for arguing with anyone else. Just don't do it. You can argue a point and within reason make yours known, and then it is either accepted or it's not.

Only give your valuable time and attention to things and people who deserve them. Continue to enjoy learning new things and meeting new people. Focus on Growth in all areas of your life. Only choose to engage in conversations with people that you know are new or that have borne fruit in the past. Lose the weight of negative people. Stay positive and keep growing. Now go forth and do great things. We wish you smooth sailing.

We will be a part of your board of directors. A Nobody Cares podcast will be up and running soon. For now, you can reach out to us directly for further guidance at badcopcoach@outlook.com

Always remember, stay focused on your goals, stay productive, and above all embrace the fact that no one cares, and no one is coming.

ABOUT THE AUTHOR

Good Cop And Bad Cop

GC BC
COACHING

Good Cop and Bad Cop have almost a combined 100 years of experience living and prospering in the western world. They also have over 50 years of combined service to the country. Between the two of them, they have served on almost every continent in the service of greater things. Both have also been through the family court experience and survived to tell the tale. They have raised or are raising men and women in their own families to find fulfillment in their traditional roles. Each of them have been in leadership roles for over 20 years and have lead thousands of men and women in the service of their country. Their pseudonyms have nothing to do with law enforcement, but everything to do with the delivery of coaching. Good Cop will give you a spoon full of sugar with your medicine. Bad Cop will cram the jagged pill down your throat while giving you a knife hand.

www.ingramcontent.com/pod-product-compliance
Lightning Source LLC
Chambersburg PA
CBHW071124280326
41935CB00010B/1105